Frommer's™

Krakow
day BY day™

1st Edition

by Peterjon Cresswell

WILEY

A John Wiley and Sons, Ltd, Publication

Contents

UK Publisher: Sally Smith
Executive Project Editor: Daniel Mersey
Commissioning Editor: Mark Henshall
Development Editor: Mark Henshall
Project Editor: Hannah Clement
Photo Research: Jill Emeny
Cartographer: John Tulip

Wiley also publishes its books in a variety of electronic formats. Some
content that appears in print may not be available in electronic books.

British Library Cataloguing in Publication Data

A catalogue record for this book is available from the British Library

ISBN: 978-0-470-69710-8

Typeset by Wiley Indianapolis Composition Services

Printed and bound in China by RR Donnelley

5 4 3 2 1

A Note from the Editorial Director

Organizing your time. That's what this guide is all about.

Other guides give you long lists of things to see and do and then expect you to fit the pieces together. The Day by Day guides are different. These guides tell you the best of everything, and then they show you how to see it *in the smartest, most time-efficient way*. Our authors have designed detailed itineraries organized by time, neighborhood, or special interest. And each tour comes with a bulleted map that takes you from stop to stop.

Hoping to take a city tour by Trabant car, climb Wawel Cathedral's Zygmunt Tower for luck or take a romantic moment on grassy slopes of the Vistula? Planning to bar hop around Plac Nowy, test out some of the city's new five-star restaurants or disappear down a bewildering salt mine? Whatever your interest or schedule, the Day by Days give you the smartest routes to follow. Not only do we take you to the top attractions, hotels, and restaurants, but we also help you access those special moments that locals get to experience—those "finds" that turn tourists into travelers.

The Day by Days are also your top choice if you're looking for one complete guide for all your travel needs. The best hotels and restaurants for every budget, the greatest shopping values, the wildest nightlife—it's all here.

Why should you trust our judgment? Because our authors personally visit each place they write about. They're an independent lot who say what they think and would never include places they wouldn't recommend to their best friends. They're also open to suggestions from readers. If you'd like to contact them, please send your comments our way at feedback@frommers.com, and we'll pass them on.

Enjoy your Day by Day guide—the most helpful travel companion you can buy. And have the trip of a lifetime.

Warm regards,

Kelly Regan

Kelly Regan, Editorial Director
Frommer's Travel Guides

About the Author

Rescued from provincial misery by football and punk rock, German-born **Peterjon Cresswell** turned to Europe for work and inspiration. He has been on the road ever since. A graduate from the University of Westminster in Russian and French, he used long-term study trips in Provence, Kiev, a Russian monastery outside Paris and Leningrad to complete theses on the French football press and the underground music scene in the Soviet Union. After joining an English-language publication, *Budapest Weeks*, he has since spent the last two decades working freelance in the region, covering sport and travel in Poland, Croatia, Germany and Slovenia. He also writes for the *Guardian*, the *Observer*, www.uefa.com, *World Soccer* and a slew of in-flight magazines. *Krakow Day by Day* is his first book for Frommer's.

Acknowledgements

The author would like to thank Piotr Art; Ewa Binkin (Polish National Tourist Office, London); Marcin Drobisz (Krakow Tourist Office); Monika Jurczyk; Ewelina Szpiech; Marcin Wojtaszek (Voytan Travel).

An Additional Note

Star Ratings, Icons & Abbreviations

Every hotel, restaurant, and attraction listing in this guide has been ranked for quality, value, service, amenities, and special features using a **star-rating system.** Hotels, restaurants, attractions, shopping, and nightlife are rated on a scale of zero stars (recommended) to three stars (exceptional). In addition to the star-rating system, we also use a **kids icon** to point out the best bets for families. Within each tour, we recommend cafes, bars or restaurants where you can take a break. Each of these stops appears in a shaded box marked with a coffee cup–shaped bullet 🍵 .

The following **abbreviations** are used for credit cards:

AE	American Express	DISC	Discover	V	Visa
DC	Diners Club	MC	MasterCard		

Frommers.com

Now that you have this guidebook to help you plan a great trip, visit our website at **www.frommers.com** for additional travel information on more than 4,000 destinations. We update features regularly to give you instant access to the most current trip-planning information available. At Frommers.com, you'll find scoops on the best airfares, lodging rates, and car rental bargains. You can even book your travel online through our reliable travel booking partners.

A Note on Prices

In the "Take a Break" and "Best Bets" sections of this book, we have used a system of dollar signs to show a range of costs for 1 night in a hotel (the price of a double-occupancy room) or the cost of an entree (main meal) at a restaurant. Use the following table to decipher the dollar signs:

Cost	Hotels	Restaurants
$	under $100	under $10
$$	$100–$200	$10–$20
$$$	$200–$300	$20–$30
$$$$	$300–$400	$30–$40
$$$$$	over $400	over $40

An Invitation to the Reader

In researching this book, we discovered many wonderful places—hotels, restaurants, shops, and more. We're sure you'll find others. Please tell us about them, so we can share the information with your fellow travelers in upcoming editions. If you were disappointed with a recommendation, we'd love to know that, too. Please write to:

Frommer's Krakow Day by Day, 1st Edition
Wiley Publishing, Inc. • 111 River St. • Hoboken, NJ 07030-577

12 Favorite
Moments

12 Favorite **Moments**

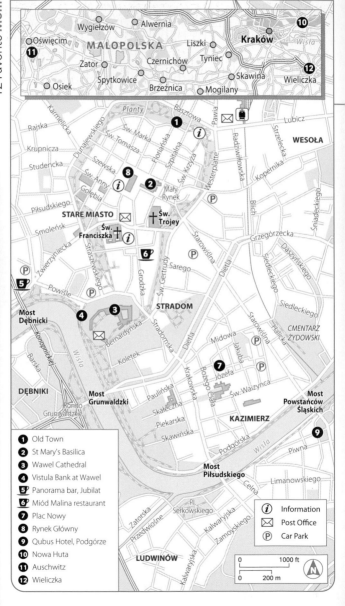

1 Old Town
2 St Mary's Basilica
3 Wawel Cathedral
4 Vistula Bank at Wawel
5 Panorama bar, Jubilat
6 Miód Malina restaurant
7 Plac Nowy
8 Rynek Główny
9 Qubus Hotel, Podgórze
10 Nowa Huta
11 Auschwitz
12 Wieliczka

(i) Information
⊠ Post Office
(P) Car Park

0   1000 ft
0   200 m

Charming, cultured, intimate Krakow is full of quirks and surprises. Who would have thought that a city with a stern historic center would have such wild nightlife? That you could tour its sights by horse and trap or Trabant car? Or that a retro shopping center would offer the best view in town from its roof-terrace restaurant? Changing rapidly as the local economy booms, Krakow's new face is reflected in every recent five-star hotel and high-end restaurant. Catch it now before the malls move in, and share some of these magic moments.

One of many glassed-in bagel stands in the city centre.

1 Starting the day with a obwarzanki bagel and taking in the Old Town. Poppy-seed, sesame or plain, the staple local bagel provides the perfect start to the day. Glassed-in stands are dotted everywhere—pick one by the Barbican and hit the Old Town like a local, bagel in hand, strolling the cobbled streets past historic façades. Not bad for a daily walk to work. *See p 44.*

2 Entering St Mary's and gawping at the ceiling. Many queue daily for Veit Stoss's main altar, but the real pleasure lies in gazing up at the ceiling as you walk in. After 600 years of war, plague, invasion and occupation, these gold stars still twinkle, the firmament as blue as blue can be. Life-affirming every time. *See p 23.*

3 Seeing the view of Krakow from the Zygmunt Tower. It's a big climb from inside Wawel Cathedral up the narrow staircase of the Zygmunt Tower—but so worth it. Stand under the clapper of the bell and touch it with your left hand for luck. *See p 9.*

4 Canoodling on the grassy slopes of the Vistula. The grassy slopes below Wawel have an unspoiled view of the Vistula. Couples canoodle over a shared can of Zywiec and the evening brings promise of nearby adventure. *See p 85.*

5 Sipping a sunset drink at the Panorama. The lift of the Jubilat shopping center whisks those in the know up to a retro club and restaurant, whose terrace offers cocktails and panoramic views. *See p 106.*

6 Tucking into top Polish cuisine at a (reserved) window seat at Miód Malina. This is the perfect spot on the Royal Route to enjoy spare ribs in honey with the house plum sauce or lamb chops in garlic and rosemary. Reliably delicious and affordable, your dish is delivered with a smile by Krakow's friendliest waiting staff. *See p 106.*

7 Barhopping around Plac Nowy. This once grim market square now boasts a dozen bars, perfect from breakfast to bedtime. *See p 58.*

8 Hearing the bugle player as you cross the market square (Rynek Glówny) late at night. Four mournful refrains float out from each corner of St Mary's tower day

Top Polish cuisine at Miód malina.

and night, whether you're shopping or clubbing. *See p 23*.

9 Sitting in the panoramic Jacuzzi atop the Qubus Hotel. The top floor of the swish Qubus comprises a glass-walled pool and Jacuzzi. Sit in the bubbles while gazing at the cityscape. *See p 144*.

10 Riding to Nowa Huta by Trabant. Krakow has tours by bike, buggy and horse-driven carriage but nothing beats a trip to retro Nowa Huta by two-stroke Trabbie. Crazy Guides run tailored visits and your own driver will talk you through social and political history as you rattle through Krakow's streets, beeped at in jest by disbelieving locals. *See p 66*.

Explore Krakow in a Crazy Guides Trabbie.

11 Seeing school groups diligently visit Auschwitz. Never again. This thought stays with you as stand beneath these gates— 'Arbeit Macht Frei'—contemplating the horrors perpetrated on the other side. School groups from across Europe stand at this same spot too, on a daily basis, before you're taken on a tour of the world's most notorious death camp. As you finish, you are all coming to the same conclusion as you board your coaches back to Krakow: never again. *See p 149*.

12 Descending the staircase of St Kinga's Chapel in Wieliczka. Halfway into a tour of Poland's most popular tourist attraction, the Salt Mine of Wieliczka outside Krakow, you reach this grand, shiny staircase, and ballroom-sized chapel below. Chandelier, altar, everything has been finely carved from rock salt by uneducated miners working for years underground. Ornate doesn't begin to describe it. *See p 20*. ●

The Best
Full-Day Tours

The Best **in One Day**

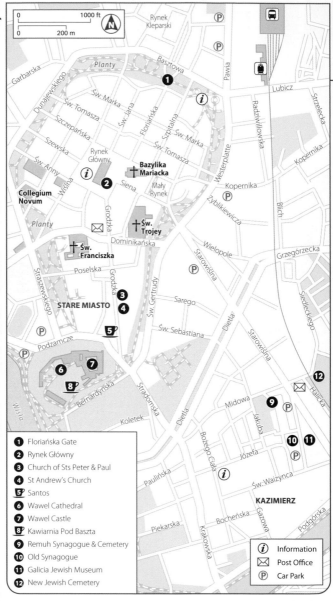

1 Floriańska Gate
2 Rynek Główny
3 Church of Sts Peter & Paul
4 St Andrew's Church
5 Santos
6 Wawel Cathedral
7 Wawel Castle
8 Kawiarnia Pod Baszta
9 Remuh Synagogue & Cemetery
10 Old Synagogue
11 Galicia Jewish Museum
12 New Jewish Cemetery

i Information
✉ Post Office
Ⓟ Car Park

This one-day tour takes in the very best of Krakow, in three key areas: the Old Town with its centerpiece of Rynek Głłówny, Europe's largest medieval square; historic hilltop Wawel, its Cathedral and Castle; and the atmospheric Jewish quarter of Kazimierz. Each treasure-filled zone is compact and walkable—the lesser landmarks you pass can be explored later at your leisure. Wear hardy shoes for Krakow's cobbled streets—no high heels. START: **All trams to Barbakan**.

1 Floriańska Gate. Enter Krakow like a king as you pass through this medieval entrance to the Old Town, one of four to survive the original 47 built in the 1300s. The Floriańska Gate forms the start of the Royal Route up to Wawel, marched by Polish monarchs and now signposted for tourists. Linked to the 15th-century Barbican bastion adjoining the tram-lined ring road around the Old Town, the Floriańska Gate bears the eagle of the Piast dynasty, rulers when the fortification was constructed. After a quick peek at the artworks mounted on the walls, join the throng down busy Floriańska up to Rynek Głłówny the main market square. 🕐 *10 min. All trams to Barbakan.*

The medieval entrance to the Old Town - Florianska Gate.

2 ★★★ kids Rynek Glówny. Take a deep breath as you arrive at

Europe's largest medieval square— the spiritual centre of Krakow and

Rynek Głłówny is Europe's largest medieval square.

Detail on the Church of Sts Peter and Paul.

the rallying point for Polish independence when the nation was off the map. Thankfully intact after the Second World War, this masterpiece of design and symmetry is strolled around by thousands of people every day. At its heart stands the Sukiennice, the former Cloth Hall now an indoor market lined with souvenir stands. Around the square are café and restaurant terraces, fashion stores and historic façades—you'll feel the urge to linger over a beer. Landmarks include St Mary's Church, the Town Hall Tower and the Kryzsztofory Palace housing the History Museum. Tourist carriages clip-clop on the cobblestones, the only transport allowed here (See Special Interest Tours: Rynek Głłówny, p 30). ⏲ *1 hr.*

❸ ★ Church of Sts Peter & Paul.

The Royal Route continues from the south-east corner of Rynek Głłówny to Grodzka, wide, historic and diverse. Halfway down the street, near the junction with Kanonicza, stands a cluster of churches. Your eye will be drawn to the most striking, the first Jesuit—and baroque—church in Krakow. Italian architects were brought over to build it in the early 1600s and, like all Jesuit churches, it is modeled on Il Gesù in Rome. Inside

the delicate stuccowork and high altar, added a century later, impress but first you'll be snapping the statues of the 12 apostles interspersed amid the railings guarding the main entrance—copies of the 18th-century originals. To one side, steps lead to the Skarga Crypt, named after the Jesuit preacher whose tombstone is dotted with wishes written by locals needing help in sundry everyday tasks. ⏲ *20 min. Grodzka 38* ☎ *012-422-65-73. www.aposto lowie.pl. Mon–Sat 9am–7pm; Sun 1.30pm–7.30pm.*

❹ ★ St Andrew's Church.

Beside Sts Peter and Paul stands this fine example of late 11th-century Romanesque architecture. Rebuilt and added to a century later, St Andrew's had its interior given a baroque makeover by the Italian architect Baldassare Fontana in the early 1700s. Amid the gilt and stucco, the pulpit, designed in the shape of a boat, stands out. ⏲ *10 min. Grodzka 56* ☎ *012-422-16-12. Daily 7.30am–5pm.*

❺ kids Santos.

Ideally situated at the bottom end of Grodzka with its tree-shaded terrace facing Wawel, this modest café and purveyor of

Snap Happy

Photos: Entering many of Krakow's churches, museums and historic attractions, the first-time visitor may not notice a special ticket price indicated at the kiosk. Buying a standard ticket and innocently snapping away happily at a rare altar or painting, said visitor may be apprehended by a steward in a luminous top—the taking of photographs requires this special ticket, usually about €3 extra. Once you've been led to the desk to buy one, you can snap away at random, send the photos to friends, post them on your blog, or show them on your living-room wall. What you can't do is publish them—the Wawel authorities are particularly scrupulous when it comes to unauthorized publication of photographs.

standard snacks and decent ice-creams provides an ideal pit-stop for those following the Royal Route. *Grodzka 65* ☎ *012-423-14-87. $.*

⑥ ★★★ Wawel Cathedral.

From the bottom of Grodzka, Wawel rises stern and historic. This fortified complex contains Poland's most precious landmarks, Wawel Castle and Cathedral, royal residence and

The historic Wawel Cathedral.

coronation site for generations of Polish monarchs. After a steep incline and two gates, you arrive at the Cathedral on your left, its ticket office opposite the main entrance. Following the arrows as you enter, your eyes are assaulted by a mass of objects and array of styles, bright chapels, ornate tombs and sarcophagi flanking the three-aisled nave. On the left-hand side is the entrance to the cathedral crypt, containing the tombs of Polish rulers and national heroes; further along, is the Zygmunt Tower. Climb the narrow, steep and claustrophobic staircase for panoramic views of Krakow. The clapper of the Zygmunt Bell, 2 metres (6.5ft) in diameter, is only used for special occasions—reach up to touch it with your left hand for luck. ⏱ *1hr 30min. Wawel 3* ☎ *012-429-33-27. www.wawel. krakow.pl. Last entry 30 min before closing. Admission 10zł/5zł. May–Sept Mon–Sat 9am–5pm, Sun 12.30pm–5pm. Oct–Apr Mon–Sat 9am–4pm, Sun 12.30pm–4pm. See p 52.*

⑦ ★★★ kids Wawel Castle.

Turning left out of the Cathedral, a short walk leads you to an elegantly

Kawiarnia Pod Baszta.

Tue–Fri 9.30am–5pm, Sat–Sun 11am–6pm. Nov–Mar Tue–Sun 9.30am–4pm. State Rooms Apr–Oct Tue–Fri 9.30am–5pm, Sat–Sun 11am–6pm. Nov–Mar Tue–Sat 10am–4pm. See p 52.

8 kids Kawiarnia Pod Baszta. Take a terrace seat to face the morning sun under Tęczyński Tower. Breakfasts until noon, soups, sandwiches, pancakes, cakes, ice-creams, standard Polish lunches, beers and spirits are served at Wawel's main café. There's a children's menu (13zł) too. *$.*

arcaded Renaissance courtyard, surrounded on three sides by a three-storey Italianate building crammed with historic treasures: Wawel Castle. Boys will enjoy the brutal medieval weaponry on show in the Crown Treasury and Armoury; grown-ups the Flemish tapestries in the State Rooms and Royal Private Apartments, accessed by guided tour only. All is housed in expansive, high-ceilinged interconnecting rooms overlooking the courtyard. As tourists shuffle in and out of this east wing, you'll see New Age practitioners making strange movements in the north-west corner. The black stone of the former St Gereon's Chapel, whose remnants are set behind the wall, is said to emanate positive energy. Facing the outer courtyard is the entrance to the medieval finds of the Lost Wawel exhibition (7zł/4zł); further on is the door to the child-friendly Dragon's Cave (3zł), a labyrinth bookended by a roaring dragon. ⏱ *1 hr 30 min. Wawel Hill.* ☎ *012-412-51-55. www.wawel.krakow.pl. Admission Treasury 14–15zł/7–8zł. Free Nov–Mar Sun. State Rooms 19–20zł/14–15zł. Treasury Apr–Oct*

9 ★★ Remuh Synagogue & Cemetery. Down Stradomska from Wawel you arrive at the Jewish quarter of Kazimierz. No longer in the Old Town, you quickly sense a different culture, its rich history and its tragic war-time loss. Turning into Miodowa, synagogues begin to spring up; a little turn into broad, square-like Szeroka and to your right is the gateway to the Remuh Synagogue and Cemetery. Founded in the 1500s and renovated in 1829, this is the only Orthodox one in Krakow still running regular religious services—Torah readings are given from the traditional bimah platform. As you exit, to your left stretches the rambling Remuh Cemetery, with the Wailing Wall immediately to the right. The inscriptions are hard to read—many gravestones were damaged when the Nazis used this for a rubbish tip. Pebbles are left on top as a mark of respect. ⏱ *1 hr. Szeroka 40* ☎ *012-429-57-35. Admission 5zł/2zł. Sun–Fri 9am–4pm. See p 27.*

10 ★★ Old Synagogue. Coming out into Szeroka, to your right at the end of the square stands the Old Synagogue, first built in the 1500s.

Burned down and rebuilt several times since, and used by the Nazis as a warehouse, it now houses the Museum of Judaism. Torah scrolls and other sacred objects line the bar interior, furnished only by an imposing bimah pulpit. Upstairs is a display of documentation relating to the Nazi occupation. ⏱ *1 hr. Szeroka 24.* ☎ *012-422-09-62. www. mhk.pl. Admission 7zł/5zł. Free Mon. Last entry 30 min before closing. Mon 10am–2pm; Tues–Sun 9am–5pm. See p 28.*

⓫ ★★ **Galicia Jewish Museum.** Recently deceased British photo-journalist Chris Schwarz (1948–2007) is behind this worthwhile exhibition, set in a converted warehouse. Aiming to broaden people's attention from the empty synagogues of Kazimierz and death factory of Auschwitz, Schwarz and writer-historian Jonathan Webber set off around southern Poland (Galicia) to record the lesser-known places of murder and massacre—a plaque in a forest clearing or a ramshackle synagogue in some forgotten village. The result, intelligently themed and starkly displayed, reflects the breadth and banality of the war crime. A bookshop, café and information point provide further reason to visit. ⏱ *30 min. Dajwór 15–23.* ☎ *012-421-68-42.*

Old Synagogue and museum.

www.galiciajewishmuseum.org. Admission 12zł/6zł. Daily 9am–7pm. See p 29.

⓬ ★★ **New Jewish Cemetery.** Over Starowislna and under the railway viaduct on Miodowa stands the gateway to Krakow's largest Jewish cemetery, the only one still in operation. Strolling around the huge site, you'll find many names from the 1800s, when this site became the main Jewish cemetery in town. By the entrance stands a monument to Jews murdered during the Second World War, built with broken tombstones. ⏱ *45 min. Miodowa 55. Mon–Thurs 10am–5pm; Fri 10am–2pm. See p 30.*

Wawel Castle from the courtyard.

The Best **in Two Days**

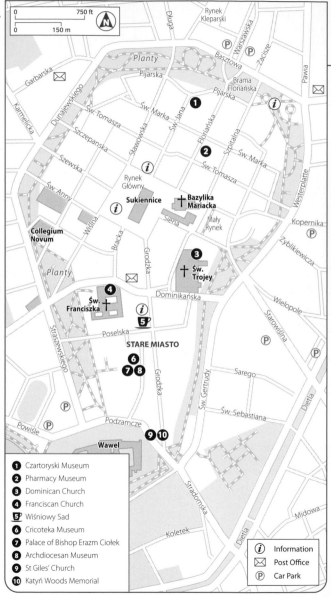

1 Czartoryski Museum
2 Pharmacy Museum
3 Dominican Church
4 Franciscan Church
5 Wiśniowy Sad
6 Cricoteka Museum
7 Palace of Bishop Erazm Ciołek
8 Archdiocesan Museum
9 St Giles' Church
10 Katyń Woods Memorial

i Information
✉ Post Office
Ⓟ Car Park

Your second day takes you right through the Old Town from top to bottom, around the historic streets of Floriańska, Grodzka and Kanonicza, part of the Royal Route to Wawel. On the way, you'll be taking in the life and works of Leonardo da Vinci (1452–1519), Pope John Paul II (1920–2005) and Tadeusz Kantor (1915–1990), Poland's legendary stage designer.

❶ ★★★ Czatoryski Museum. One of Krakow's most remarkable museums contains Da Vinci's, *Lady with an Ermine*, Spanish, Venetian and Flemish pieces, and military paraphernalia from all over Europe. Pick up a handy English-language audio guide. 🕐 *1 1/2 hr. Św Jana 19* ☎ *012-422-55-66. Admission 10zł/5zł. Free Thurs. May–Oct Tue, Thur 10am–4pm, Wed, Fri, Sat 10am–7pm, Sun 10am–3pm. Nov–Apr Tue, Thur, Sat–Sun 10am–3.30pm, Wed, Fri 10am–6pm. See p 45.*

❷ ★★ kids Pharmacy Museum. The quirky, surprising Pharmacy Museum fills this 15th-century building, each floor representing an apothecary from a

Czatoryski Museum.

particular century. You'll get a better feel here for how locals lived than at any other standard museum. 🕐 *1 hr. Floriańska 25* ☎ *012-421-92-79. Admission 6zł/3zł. Tue noon–6.30pm. Wed–Sun 10am–2.30pm. See p 46.*

❸ ★ Dominican Church. Of all the churches in Krakow, the Dominican attracts the most faithful congregation—mass here really is a thing to behold. Founded by the Dominicans in 1250, this pretty mishmash of a church is a late 19th-century rebuild of the 13th-century Gothic original. Look out for the Myszkowski Chapel, its dome dotted with family busts. 🕐 *30 min. Stolarska 12* ☎ *012-423-16-13. Daily 8am–8pm. See p 47.*

❹ ★ Franciscan Church. Fire, fashion and Swedish invasions are responsible for the varied architectural styles of this large church and cloisters. For its near eight centuries of history, baroque, neo-Romanesque and neo-Gothic aspects, the Franciscan Church is best known for the interior work of Stanisław Wyspiański (1869–1907). Light floods in through the Art Nouveau forms of his stained-glass creations on each of the north and south wings—flowers, stars and swirling patterns against a blue background. He was also responsible for the murals in the choir. Portraits of every Krakow bishop to the present day line the Gothic cloister. 🕐 *30 min. Wszystkich Świętych* ☎ *012-422-53-76. Mon–Sat 10am–4.30pm.*

5 **Wiśniowy Sad.** Russian specialties—borscht, solyanka (a rich, spicy stew), blini with caviar—complement a decent range of chilled vodkas at the Cherry Orchard, accessed down a quaint Grodzka passageway. *Grodzka 33.* ☎ *012-430-21-11. $.*

6 ★ **Cricoteka Museum.** The former home of Tadeusz Kantor's groundbreaking theatre Cricot 2 now contains an eclectic archive of his work—to call it a museum is doing it an injustice. Costumes, videos, drawings, designs, journals, photos, testify to the craft and imagination of Poland's greatest stage designer of the 20th century. Kantor himself put the house together before his death in 1990, a legacy in the 'minds and imagination for the coming generations'. For those unfamiliar with his work, it's the range of materials that strikes most—every Kantor production must have been a complete surprise. ⏲ *20 min. Kanonicza 5* ☎ *012-422-83-32. July–Aug Daily 10am–4pm. Sept–June Mon–Fri 10am–4pm.*

Dominican Church.

7 ★ **Palace of Bishop Erazm Ciołek.** Overhauled and reopened in the summer of 2008, this two-part collection covers the first era of a panoramic overview of Polish art—the 18th- and 19th-century section (currently under renovation) is at the Sukiennice (p 24), the 20th at the National Museum (p 19). Here, in the sumptuous early 16th-century palace of canon, diplomat and arts patron Bishop Erazm Ciołek, you'll find a gallery of Old Polish art between the 12th and 18th centuries, and another of orthodox art. The former features the late 15th century Gothic works of Veit Stoss (c1445–1533), responsible for the High Altar at St Mary's Basilica (p 23), and ecclesiastical works of the Renaissance and baroque periods. The highlights are the icons of Ruthenia, the Balkans and the 17th-century Poland, vibrant Byzantine images of Christ and the Virgin. The historic setting and striking interiors round out the experience. ⏲ *40 min. Kanonicza 17* ☎ *012-429-15-58. Admission Combined 20zł/10zł. Old Polish 12zł/6zł. Orthodox 6zł/3zł.90. Free Sun. Tue–Sat 10am–6pm, Sun 10am–4pm.*

Stunning detail from the Palace of Bishop Erazm Ciolek.

8 ★ Archdiocesan Museum.
The life, work and travels of Pope John Paul II are the main subject here—temporary exhibitions of church art are often staged as well. Upstairs begins with a map of Papal pilgrimages, moving on to his skull caps, cloaks, amateur paintings, airline schedules with Alitalia, bicycles and even his canoe. A goalkeeper for local football club Cracovia, John Paul was a man of sport too. Gifts from around the world are also on display, salvers, figurines and a beautifully hand-painted chess set from the President of Uruguay. There's also a reconstruction of the room he lived in while working here—the original is in the adjoining Deanery. ⏲ *20 min. Kanonicza 19* ☎ *012-421-89-63. Admission 5zł/3zł. Tue–Fri 10am–4pm, Sat–Sun 10am–3pm.*

9 ★ St Giles' Church. The last stop on the Royal Route before Wawel, St Giles' has a rather patchwork history. Founded in 1082, it was rebuilt in the early 1300s and acquired its present appearance in the early 1600s. An English-language Catholic mass is given here on Sunday mornings; many visit for the summer concerts too. ⏲ *15 min. Św.Idziego 1. Daily.*

10 Katyń Woods Memorial.
Erected in 1990, the crucifix in the cobbled square outside St Giles' reads: 'Katyń 1940–1990'. The mass execution of 20,000 Polish officers and policemen by Stalin in the Katyń woods near Smolensk was covered up for decades. By the late 1980s, then leader Gorbachëv was under pressure to admit Soviet guilt — acknowledged on 13 April 1990, the anniversary of the discovery of the mass graves by the Nazis in 1943. This stark memorial crucifix was erected afterwards. ⏲ *15 min. Św.Idziego.*

Archdiocesan Museum.

The Best **Full-Day Tours**

The Best **in Three Days**

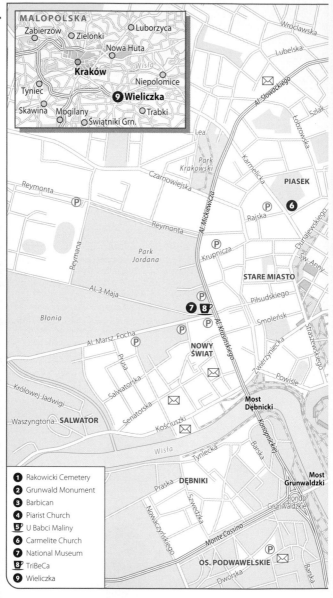

MALOPOLSKA

Zabierzów · Zielonki · Luborzyca

Nowa Huta

Kraków · Wisła

Tyniec · Niepolomice

9 Wieliczka

Skawina · Mogilany · Trabki

Świątniki Grn.

Wrocławska
Lubelska
Al. Słowackiego
Szlak
Lobzowska

Reymonta
Park Krakowski
Karmelicka
PIASEK
(P) · Rajska · **6**
Reymonta

Park Jordana
(P) Krupnicza
STARE MIASTO
Piłsudskiego
Smoleńsk

Al. 3-Maja
7 8
(P)
NOWY ŚWIAT
Powiśle

Błonia
Al. Marsz. Focha
(P)
Zwierzyniecka

Pusta
Salwatorska
Most Dębnicki

Królowej-Jadwigi
Senatorska
Kościuszki

Waszyngtona **SALWATOR**
Wisła · Tyniecka
Most Grunwaldzki

DĘBNIKI
Praska · Barska
Fondo Grunwaldzkie

① Rakowicki Cemetery
② Grunwald Monument
③ Barbican
④ Piarist Church
⑤ U Babci Maliny
⑥ Carmelite Church
⑦ National Museum
⑧ TriBeCa
⑨ Wieliczka

Monte Cassino
(P)
OS. PODWAWELSKIE
Dworska
Barska

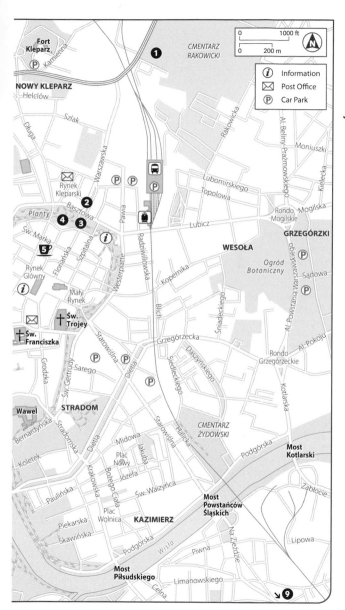

0	1000 ft
0	200 m

ⓘ Information
✉ Post Office
Ⓟ Car Park

Fort Kleparz
Ⓟ Kamienna
CMENTARZ RAKOWICKI

NOWY KLEPARZ
Helclów

Rakowicka
Al. Beliny-Prażmowskiego
Moniuszki
Kielecka

Szlak
Warszawska
Długa

Ⓟ Ⓟ Ⓟ
Lubomirskiego
Topolowa

✉ Rynek Kleparski
Basztowa
Pawia
Lubicz
Rondo Mogilskie
Mogilska
GRZEGÓRZKI

Planty
Sw. Marka
Floriańska
Szpitala
Westerplatte
Radziwiłłowska
Kopernika
WESOŁA
Ogród Botaniczny
Sądowa
Ⓟ

ⓘ
Rynek Główny
ⓘ
Mały Rynek
Bhich
Śniadeckiego
Al. Powstania Warszawskiego

✉
✝ Sw. Trojey
Grzegórzecka
Daszyńskiego
Siedleckiego
Rondo Grzegórzeckie
Al. Pokoju
Kotlarska

✝ Sw. Franciszka
Grodzka
Sw. Gertrudy
Sarego
Ⓟ
Dietla
Ⓟ
Starowiślna

Wawel
STRADOM
Bernardyńska
Stradomska
Dietla
Midowa
Jakuba
Starowiślna
Halicka
CMENTARZ ŻYDOWSKI
Podgórska
Most Kotlarski

Koletek
Krakowska
Plac Nowy
Bożego Ciała
Józefa
Sw. Wawrzyńca
Most Powstańców Śląskich
Zabłocie

Paulińska
Plac Wolnica
KAZIMIERZ
Na Zjeździe
Lipowa

Piekarska
Skawińska
Podgórska
Wisła
Piwna

Most Piłsudskiego
Limanowskiego
Celna
↘ 9

Day three leads you from the Old Town to discover the key sights an easy hop away. Skirting the pretty Planty (p 88) and erudite University Quarter (p 48), you can explore a couple of Krakow's most attractive and unusual churches in more detail before delving into the National Museum and its unsurpassed collection of post-war Polish art. From the nearby Hotel Cracovia, tourist buses leave for Wieliczka, a unique underground labyrinth lined with statues made completely from salt—the most popular visitor attraction in Poland.

❶ Rakowicki Cemetery.

Krakow's biggest cemetery occupies a vast tract just north of the main train station, a treasure of 19th-century funerary architecture and the resting place of some of Poland's greatest figures 19th century artists Józef Mehoffer (1869–1946) and Jan Matejko (1838–1893), war-time Ghetto pharmacist Tadeusz Pankiewicz (1908–1993) and 20th century theatre director Tadeusz Kantor, they're all here. If you're in town around All Souls' Day, November 1, a visit here is memorable, candles in translucent colored vases creating halos of light all around. ⏱ *1 hr. Ul.Rakowicka. Trams 2: Rakowicka n/z.*

❷ Grunwald Monument. Ten

minutes' walk towards the Old Town, this imposing depiction of Poland's greatest victory on the battlefield is a copy of the 1910 original, which was demolished by the Nazis. For Germans, Grunwald is Tannenberg, the great military defeat for the Teutonic Knights at the hands of Poland and Lithuania 500 years before this monument was unveiled. The figures dramatically arrayed are the victorious King Jagiella and the fallen Teutonic leader, surrounded by knights and solders. Centerpiecing plac Matejki, the work aligns neatly with Barbican and the Royal Route down Floriańska. ⏱ *10 min. Plac Matejki. All trams to Dworzec Główny.*

Grunwald Monument on Matejki Square.

❸ ★ Barbican. Fears of Turkish

invasion led to the construction of this once mighty fortress and drawbridge in the late 1400s. Surrounded by a huge moat, the Barbican was never put to its original use—the Turks never came. The seven turrets and loopholes arranged at various levels are said to relate to astrological symbolism popular at the time. Today its grassed-over surrounds allow for a pleasant stroll into the Old Town from the north, linked to the Floriańska Gate (p 7) and the shopping stretch of Floriańska. The Barbican is used for exhibitions, concerts its own festival of classical music in June. *20 min. Basztowa. All trams to Basztowa.*

4 ★ Piarist Church. A grand Rococo façade andan equally ornate baroque interior with trompe l'oeil frescoes add an Italianate touch to this church at the far end of Floriańska—designer Kasper Bażanka was trained in Rome under Andrea Pozzo, Jesuit virtuoso of the illusionist mural. At Easter, the crypt is opened to display an intricate model of Christ's Tomb, usually with contemporary undertones. *20 min. Pijarska 2 ☎ 012-422-22-55. Free admission. Daily. All trams to Basztowa.*

5 U Babci Maliny. Favorite fill-up pierogi (Slavic dumplings) place for many a local. Cheap, hearty helpings of pierogi doughballs of various fillings are served seven days a week in a rustic basement. *Ul. Stawkowska ☎ 012-422-76-01. $.*

6 ★ Carmelite Church. Also known as the Church on the Sand, this was the spot where the 11th-century Duke of Poland Władysław Herman discovered a pile of sand used to heal a terrible pox on his legs. His legacy of a votive church didn't last the Swedish invasions, so this baroque one was erected in the 17th century. An icon of the Madonna of the Sand covers one wall. Of recent note has been the renovation of the two-room sacristy to its former glory, altar, cabinets, chandelier and all. *30 min. Karmelicka 19 ☎ 012-632-67-52. Daily 9.30am–4.30pm, 5pm–7pm.*

7 ★★ National Museum. Modern Polish art, decorative art and military paraphernalia fill each of three floors in this functional pre-war edifice by a major intersection west of the Old Town. You can buy a ticket for all three floors, or one for the 20th-century art separately. The ground floor is given over to temporary exhibitions and a permanent

The Barbican.

one of weapons and uniforms: the 'Arms and Colours in Poland'. Highlights include the tunic of World War I hero József Piłsudski, a golden baton from the Battle of Vienna of 1683, and a spearhead found on the battlefield at Grunwald. One floor up are the 4,000 exhibits of the Gallery of Decorative Arts, ecclesiastical stained glass, historic ladies' dresses, ceramics and numerous ornate boxes. A 10th-century wrought-silver goblet, found at Włocławek, takes pride of place. Focus falls on the Młoda Polska and Grupa Krakowska movements (of modernist visual art) in the top-floor section, where works by Józef Mehoffer, Tadeusz Kantor and Stanisław Wyspiański highlight the importance of the late 19th and 20th century cultural life. ⏱ *2 hr. Al.3 Maja 1* ☎ *012-633-53-31. Admission Combined 20zł/10zł. Arms & Colours/ Decorative Arts 6zł/3zł. 20th-Century Polish Art 10zł/5zł. Free May–Oct Sun. Free Nov–Apr Thur. May–Oct Tue–Sat 10am–6pm, Sun 10am–4pm. Nov–Apr Tue, Thur, Sun 10am–3.30pm, Wed, Fri, Sat 10am–6pm. All trams to Cracovia.*

8 **TriBeCa** In the lobby of the National Museum, this chic café is a cut above. Arabica coffee from Guatemala, chocolatinis, obscure fruit smoothies, focaccia sandwiches, toasts and tramezzini, all are served in stylish surroundings under a sea-scene ceiling. *Al.3 Maja 1* ☎ *012-633-53-31. $.*

9 ★★★ **kids** **Wieliczka.** Poland's busiest tourist site means queues outside the main building and wait for the 36-person lift to come rattling up to ground level, even if you've booked a timed guided tour from Krakow. Your visit to the Wieliczka Mine lasts two hours, through a labyrinth of corridors, where salt was mined for centuries. Exhibits cover mining techniques and equipment, and the figures intricately carved by the miners during their years underground. Most notable is the Chapel of St Kinga, a 400m^2 hall accessed down a (slippery) grand staircase, lit by a vast chandelier. Occasionally the tour lapses into kitsch—Chopin playing to a light show—but Wieliczka proves a winner with all the family. Be prepared to descend a lot of stairs. ⏱ *2 hr. Ul.Daniłowicza 10, Wieliczka* ☎ *012-278-73-02. www.kopalnia.pl Admission 63zł/48zł or with tour group. Daily 7.30am–7.30pm. All trains/ minibuses to Wieliczka or by regular guided tour.* ●

Relaxing outside the National Museum.

Rynek **Główny**

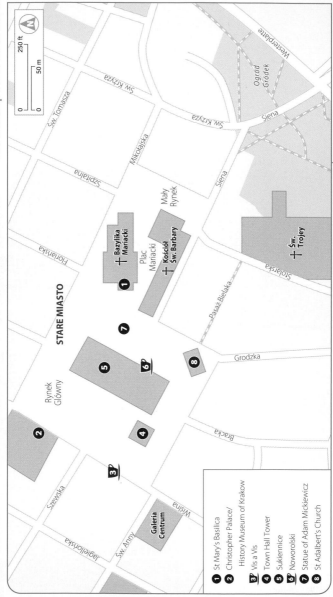

STARE MIASTO

Rynek Główny

Plac Mariacki

Mały Rynek

† **Bazylika Mariacki**

† **Kościół Św. Barbary**

† **Św. Trojey**

Galeria Centrum

Św. Tomasza
Św. Krzyża
Mikołajska
Szpitalna
Florianśka
Św. Krzyża
Siena
Siena
Ogród Gródek
Westerplatte
Stolarska
Pasaż Bielaka
Grodzka
Bracka
Wiślna
Szewska
Św. Anny
Jagiellońska

250 ft
50 m
0
0

❶ St Mary's Basilica
❷ Christopher Palace/
   History Museum of Kraków
❸ Vis a Vis
❹ Town Hall Tower
❺ Sukiennice
❻ Noworolski
❼ Statue of Adam Mickiewicz
❽ St Adalbert's Church

Mercifully untouched by war or 1970s' developers, the showpiece main market square of Rynek Główny glitters from all four sides with the grand neo-Classical façades of the 18th and 19th-centuries. Towering over the 200 m by 200 m flagstone surface are four historic buildings: the stand-out Gothic St Mary's Basilica and its historic high altar; the centerpiece Sukiennice Cloth Hall; the Town Hall Tower and St Adalbert's Church. Surrounding them, two dozen terrace cafés, landmark restaurants and upmarket boutiques are arranged according to the square's neat, alphabetical order—row A–B for the north flank, and so on. Over a constantly moving tableau of strolling pedestrians, street performers and clip-clopping carriages, a lone bugler marks every hour from atop St Mary's with a signal tune.

❶ ★★★ **St Mary's Basilica.** The jewel in Krakow's crown and one of the great works of the Gothic era. St Mary's is fronted by two towers, the taller one bearing a spire and attracting everyone's attention on the hour when a trumpeter plays a bugle call four times, a tradition dating back to the Tatar invasion of 1241. Get your ticket from the office opposite the visitors' entrance round the corner on plac Mariacki and find a pew beneath the blue-starred ceiling by 11.50am (not Sundays), before the six hinged wings of Veit Stoss's masterful High Altar (1477-1489) are unfolded for their daily public view. Some 11 metres long and 12 metres high, the altar is huge, its central section painstakingly depicting the Assumption of the Virgin. The realistic features on the faces of the Apostles are uncanny —the young Stoss was said to have taken them from real-life characters. The wings show scenes from Christ's life—the Nativity, Resurrection, and so on. The most prominent Polish artists here of the 19th century – were responsible for many of the stained-glass designs and murals in the nave. ⏱ *1 hr. Arrive Mon–Sat before 11.40am for the altar opening at 11.50am. Plac Mariacki 5* ☎ *012-422-05-21.*

The stunning ceiling in St Mary's Basilica.

Admission 6zł/3zł. Mon–Sat 11.30am–6pm, Sun 2pm–6pm.

❷ ★ **Christopher Palace/ History Museum of Krakow.** The grand Christopher Palace owes its present appearance to a remodel in the 1680s. Frequented by various cultural societies over the years, it is best known for hosting meetings of influential post-war artists, the Grupa Krakowska. Today its main function is to accommodate the History Museum of Krakow, much of

Climb the 100-step staircase for a bird's eye view of Rynek Główny.

which is under renovation until 2009. ⏱ *40 min. Rynek Główny 35* ☎ *012-619-23-00. Admission 8zł/5zł. Wed–Sun 10am–5.30pm.*

3⃣ Vis a Vis. Rynek Główny's most unpretentious bar is a suitable spot for Piotr Skryznecki (1930–1997) to pose. Founder of the cabaret at the Piwnica pod Baranami, the most groundbreaking of its day, Skryznecki was a regular at this simple but friendly stand-up locals' bar. In summer, sit outside, a chance for the seated Skryznecki, now in statue form over a decade after his death, roses in hand, to catch up on all the gossip. *Rynek Główny 29* ☎ *012-422-69-61. $.*

4⃣ ★ Town Hall Tower. Once part of a 14th-century town hall, the remaining tower has been converted into a modest museum and simple main-square attraction. A model of the original town hall and vintage photographs from the Old Town form the bulk of the exhibition, but most come here to scale the giddying 100-step staircase for a birds' eye view of the square below. Outside at street level, a plaque marks where Colonel Bolesław Roja claimed power from the Austrian authorities in 1918, thus gaining Poland independence after 123 years. ⏱ *20 min. Rynek Główny 1* ☎ *012-619-23-20. Admission 5zł/3.50zł. May–Oct Daily 10.30am–2pm, 2.30pm–6pm.*

5⃣ ★ Sukiennice. Rynek Główny's centerpiece has been a place of trade for seven centuries. Where there was once cloth-cutting and artisans are

Buy your souvenirs at Sukiennice.

Noworolski.

⑦ Statue of Adam Mickiewicz. Mickiewicz never came to Krakow but Poland's national poet has been awarded a crucial role in the daily life of the city—his statue outside the Sukiennice is the most popular meeting place in Krakow. The monument is in fact a remake, the original was destroyed in the Second World War, and has allegorical figures sitting at the feet of the man responsible for the greatest poetic epic of Polish letters, 'Pan Tadeusz'. Mickiewicz himself had a sad life, living during the era of Polish partition and suffering two periods of exile, in Moscow and Paris. After his death in Istanbul, his body was brought to Wawel Cathedral for burial. 🕒 *10 min.*

now traders of souvenirs and overpriced jewellery. Nonetheless the building itself, given a neo-Gothic makeover, colonnades and all, in the 1870s, beckons you to walk through and browse with scores of other tourists. By 2010 the upstairs painting gallery, filled with Polish works from the 19th century and a branch of the National Museum, will be reopened after extensive renovation. 🕒 *20 min.*

Statue of Adam Mickiewicz.

⑧ ★ St Adalbert's Church. Surrounded by the pristine symmetry of the main market square, this, the oldest building on it, sticks out like a sore thumb. First, it is a complete jumble of styles, partly Romanesque, partly baroque, after various remakes in over a thousand years of service. During that time, the market square has been paved over and added to, leaving St Adalbert's still set at the its original level, at least 2 m lower than today's Rynek Główny. It's also tiny, the smallest church in Krakow, topped with a somewhat grandiose dome. Such a venerable anomaly is almost impossible to resist, although once you're inside, the sundry collection of archaeological finds on display will merit just a quick perusal. 🕒 *30 min. Rynek Główny* ☎ *012-422-83-52. Mon–Sat 9am–5pm, Sun 1.30pm–5pm.*

⑥ Noworolski. You won't find a more inspiring spot to write your postcards.than this grand café, tucked in the Sukiennice. With outdoor tables in its arcades, it has seen many a famous regular—Lenin for one. The sumptuous fin-de-siècle interior gives you the impression of sitting inside a wedding cake, decoration, location and heritage allowing the management to charge three times the going rate for coffee. Breakfasts, salads, cakes, soups and main courses are all quite reasonably priced on the terrace, though. *Rynek Główny 1/3* ☎ *012-422-47-71. $$.*

Jewish **Krakow**

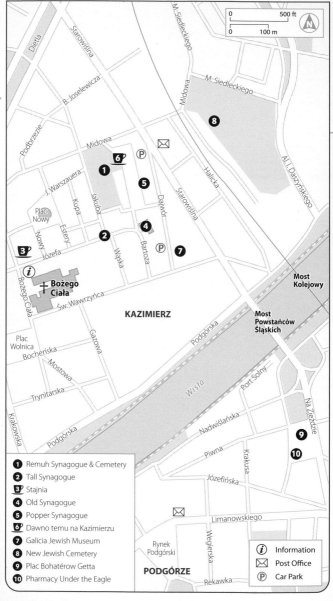

1 Remuh Synagogue & Cemetery
2 Tall Synagogue
3 Stajnia
4 Old Synagogue
5 Popper Synagogue
6 Dawno temu na Kazimierzu
7 Galicia Jewish Museum
8 New Jewish Cemetery
9 Plac Bohatérow Getta
10 Pharmacy Under the Eagle

(i) Information
⊠ Post Office
Ⓟ Car Park

Krakow's Jews have been settled in Kazimierz since the end of the 14th century. Tradesmen, publishers and butchers, the community thrived in a sectioned-off area bordered by Józefa, the street leading to Kazimierz's Christian quarter. The walls came down in the 1800s, and as Jews and Christians mixed, a rich cultural life flourished. The Nazi invasion saw Jews forcibly herded into a ghetto designated for them across the river in Podgórze, the site of horrendous atrocities. After decades of neglect, the recent renovation of Kazimierz's synagogues and revival of Jewish culture is a much welcomed phenomenon, and have helped make Kazimierz the most vibrant district in the city.

❶ ★★ Remuh Synagogue & Cemetery.

It is apt that any tour of Jewish Krakow should start here, for the Remuh is its spiritual heart. Founded in 1553, the Remuh was known as the 'New' Synagogue as it followed the 'Old' one nearby. It was named after Moses Isserles (1520–1572), or 'Remuh', son of the founder and Chief Rabbi of Krakow in the 1500s. Its appearance changed with renovations in 1829 and 1933, and with the Nazi destruction soon after. Much of the modest interior—the bimah platform, the wall tablets—were rebuilt after the war. The Remuh is still a working house of prayer. Thousands of Jews from around the world flock to the rambling Remuh Cemetery, the gateway to your left as you leave the synagogue. Containing some of the oldest Jewish tombs in Poland, the cemetery was battered and used as a rubbish tip by the Nazis—most of today's stones were excavated after the war. Pebbles are left on top as a mark of respect. Broken fragments were used to make a Wailing Wall to the right as you enter the hallowed ground. Sadly much of the far area flanked by

Remuh Cemetary, founded in 1553.

The Old Synagogue houses a museum of Judaism.

Miodowa and Jakuba is stlll unkempt and shabby. ⏱ *1 hr. Szeroka 40* ☎ *012-429-57-35. Admission 5zł/2zł. Sun–Fri 9am–4pm. Trams 9, 13, 24, 34: Miodowa.*

2 Tall Synagogue. A sharp turn right onto Jozefa at the other end of Szeroka stands what is know as the Tall Synagogue. Named 'Tall' as its prayer rooms were on the first floor, above a row of shops supported by four buttresses, this was the third synagogue to open in Krakow. The bulk of its murals and furnishings did not survive the Second World War, but gradual restoration has seen the Wysoka slowly come back to life. It currently houses an exhibition relating to a well-known Yiddish production by famed director Andrzej Wajda (1926–)—a theatre was set up next door in the 1960s. The most prominent other feature here is the 17th-century portal on the opposite side of the otherwise bare main room. ⏱ *15 min. Józefa 38* ☎ *012-426-75-20. Admission 9zł/6zł. Summer Sun–Fri 9am-7pm. Winter Sun–Fri 9am-5pm. Trams 9, 13, 24, 34: Miodowa.*

3 Stajnia. There is little wrong with the pierogi, pizzas and salads served at 'the Stable' pub—but its hallowed place on any tour of Jewish Krakow is due to its surrounding courtyard, one of the most memorable sets used by Steven Spielberg when filming *Schindler's List*. Chairs and tables fill the open space. *Józefa 12.* ☎ *021-423-72-02. $.*

4 ★★ Old Synagogue. Poland's oldest surviving synagogue and historic seat of the local Jewish authorities, this large, red-brick building was converted to a Museum of Judaism after its war-time destruction. Founded in the early 1400s—no-one knows exactly when—the synagogue was rebuilt with Renaissance touches in 1570 after one of several fires, and added to over the centuries. Displays in its two-floor permanent exhibition cover local Jewish life and culture—shawls, yarmulke caps and various ceremonial items are well presented and explained in English. Particular accent is placed on education—the layman gets a good idea of what it was like to grow up in this community a century ago. The striking bimah platform is a reconstruction—the original staged many historic speeches, including one by Polish national hero Tadeusz Kościuszko (1746–1817) in 1794 urging Jews to join the Uprising. Upstairs is a display of documentation relating to the Nazi occupation. 🕐 *1 hr. Szeroka 24.* ☎ *012-422-09-62. www.mhk.pl. Admission 7zł/5zł. Last entry 30 min before closing. Mon 10am–2pm; Tues–Sun 9am–5pm. Free Mon. Trams 3, 9, 11, 13, 24: Wawrzyńca.*

5 Popper Synagogue. Today an arts studio used by local children, the Popper Synagogue is part of the rich oral history of Jewish Kazimierz. It was named after Wolf Popper, a financier of the early 1600s, nicknamed 'the Stork' after his habit of standing on one leg while addressing people. This was Krakow's most lavish synagogue, until its inevitable destruction at the hands of the Nazis. Its modern-day use lends it a colorful, lively atmosphere—bright banners usually decorate the inner courtyard as you walk through the main entrance between a stretch of landmark restaurants on focal Szeroka. 🕐 *15 min. Szeroka 16* ☎ *012-421-29-87. Admission Free. Trams 9, 13, 24, 34: Miodowa.*

6 Dawno temu na Kazimierzu. 'Once Upon a Time in Kazimierz' is both a historic reconstruction of the shops and workshops that thrived in this building before the war, and a comfortable spot to tuck into specialties such as onion soup with caramel, duck fillet in cranberry sauce or a stiff glass of Kosher vodka. *Szeroka 1* ☎ *021-421-21-17. $.*

7 ★★ Galicia Jewish Museum. Recently deceased British photojournalist Chris Schwarz (1948–2007) is behind this thought-provoking exhibition, set in a converted warehouse. Aiming to broaden people's attention from the empty synagogues of Kazimierz and the death factory of Auschwitz, Schwarz and writer-historian Jonathan Webber

The monument by the entrance of the New Jewish Cemetery.

set off around southern Poland (Galicia) to record the lesser-known places of murder and massacre—a plaque in a forest clearing or a ramshackle synagogue in some forgotten village. The result, intelligently themed and starkly displayed, offers some idea of the breadth and banality of the war crime. A bookshop, café and information point provide further reason to visit. ⏲ *30 min. Dajwór 15–23.* ☎ *012-421-68-42. www.galiciajewishmuseum.org. Admission 12zł/6zł. Daily 9am–7pm. Trams 3, 9, 11, 13, 24: Wawrzyńca.*

⑧ ★★ New Jewish Cemetery. Over Starowiślna and under the railway viaduct on Miodowa stands the gateway to Krakow's largest Jewish cemetery, which opened as the Remuh closed in the early 1800s. As such, it houses some of the most prominent figures of Jewish life before the Second World War— poets, politicians, photographers— but the post-war renovation of this huge, overgrown site is still a long way from completion. It is still a working place of burial, new tombs found close to the railway line. By the entrance stands a monument to Jews murdered during the war, built with broken tombstones, a sharp and striking reminder of how the cemetery must have looked when discovered in 1945. ⏲ *45 min. Miodowa 55. Mon–Thurs 10am–5pm; Fri 10am–2pm. Trams 3, 9, 11, 13, 24: Miodowa.*

⑨ ★ Plac Bohaterów Getta. A grey square just over the river from Kazimierz, 'Heroes of the Ghetto Square' was once Plac Zgody, at the northern edge of the war-time Jewish Ghetto. This was where Jews were rounded up before being sent to concentration camps, and the site of an appalling Nazi massacre in March 1943. Today it is dotted with 70 chairs, the contemporary installation by Piotr Lewicki and Kazimierz Łatak harking back to the time when Jews had to discard their furniture before being sent to their death. The focus on such everyday items brings home the evil of the heinous crimes committed here. Now lined by new shops and businesses, the

Plac Bohaterów Getta.

square features signposts and maps indicating the main sites of the Jewish Ghetto and, in one corner, the Pharmacy Under the Eagle museum. 🕐 *15 min. Trams 9, 13, 24, 34: Pl.Boh.Getta.*

⑩ ★★ Pharmacy Under the Eagle. A place in history for this former working pharmacy is assured, thanks to the brave work of its owner, Tadeusz Pankiewicz. Converted to a museum in 1983, the Apteka Pod Orłem, the only pharmacy in the Jewish Ghetto set up by the Nazis in 1941, became a secret resource and meeting place for Jews attempting to survive the atrocities. Their activities, selflessly facilitated by Pankiewicz, are illustrated and documented in three rooms here, in the form of film footage, original artifacts and explanations in four languages. Particularly harrowing are the descriptions of people who sought escape through the sewers—others falling and drowning—to an uncertain fate at the other end. Note also the letters of gratitude sent by various Jewish organizations to Pankiewicz after the war. 🕐 *30 min. 18 Plac Bohaterów Getta* ☎ *012-656-56-25. Admission 5zł*

Pharmacy Under the Eagle.

adults 4zł students. Free Mondays. Apr–Oct Mon 10am–2pm, Tues–Sun 9.30am–5pm. Nov–Mar Mon 10am–2pm, Tues–Thurs, Sat 9am–4pm, Fri 10am–5pm. Closed first Tues of the month. Trams 9, 13, 24, 34: Pl.Boh,Getta.

Mind Your Head

Yarmulke: All male visitors to sacred Jewish sites must wear the yarmulke traditional skullcap as a sign of reverence. In Krakow, this is particularly required at the two main Jewish cemeteries. At the Remuh, a man will hand men a yarmulke (a Yiddish word possibly of Polish origin) from a bag of them at the door to the synagogue. At the New Cemetery, a girl might dash out from the funeral house by the gate and hand you one. If no yarmulke is immediately to hand, don't just breeze in regardless—a supply will be put out somewhere by the entrance.

War-time **Krakow**

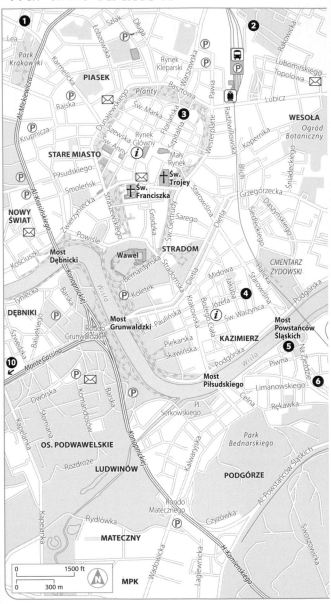

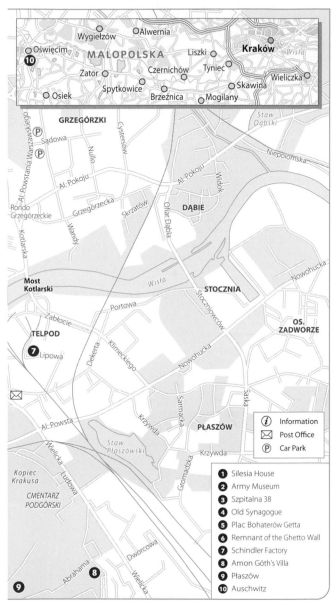

Malopolska region map showing: Wygiełzów, Alwernia, Oświęcim 10, Zator, Liszki, Kraków, Czernichów, Tyniec, Wieliczka, Osiek, Spytkowice, Brzeźnica, Skawina, Mogilany

Kraków city map showing districts: GRZEGÓRZKI, DĄBIE, STOCZNIA, OS. ZADWORZE, TELPOD, PŁASZÓW, Stocznia, and streets including Al. Powstania Warszawskiego, Sądowa, Nullo, Cystersów, Al. Pokoju, Grzegórzecka, Skrzatów, Widok, Ofiar Dąbia, Niepolomska, Nowohucka, Kotlarska, Rondo Grzegórzeckie, Wandy, Most Kotlarski, Wisła, Portowa, Stoczniowców, Zabłocie, Lipowa, Deperta, Klimeckiego, Nowohucka, Sarnacka, Saska, Al. Powsta, Krzywda, Wielicka, Ludowa, Kopiec Krakusa, Staw Płaszówski, Gromadzka, Krzywda, CMENTARZ PODGÓRSKI, Abrahama, Dworcowa, Wielicka

Staw Dąbski, Staw Płaszówski

ⓘ	Information
✉	Post Office
Ⓟ	Car Park

1. Silesia House
2. Army Museum
3. Szpitalna 38
4. Old Synagogue
5. Plac Bohaterów Getta
6. Remnant of the Ghetto Wall
7. Schindler Factory
8. Amon Göth's Villa
9. Płaszów
10. Auschwitz

Although Krakow was spared war-time bombing, its role as the seat of the Nazi Governor General saw its citizens suffer grim repression and torture. The Jewish community in Kazimierz was herded into a ghetto across the river in Podgórze, from where many were sent to the camps at nearby Płaszów and Auschwitz. Resistance, most notably by factory owner Oskar Schindler and phamarcist Tadeusz Pankiewicz, has since become the stuff of legend. Evidence of the Nazi era is scattered over remote parts of the city, some obscure and overgrown, some converted for public viewing.

❶ ★★ Silesia House. An unprepossessing building by the northwest corner of Krakow's outer ring road, this was the Gestapo headquarters during the war. From the outer wall, hands reach out from prison bars, a striking sculpture set by the main gate into a non-descript courtyard. Press the bell immediately to your right and someone skips down from one of the flats to lead you into a basement. You're handed an English-language text and shown four tiny rooms—torture cells, with the original graffiti still carved on the walls, desperate messages ('21.XI.1944—fifth day of beating') left behind after 65 years. Upstairs, a more conventional exhibition displays the activities of the Jewish Fighting Organization (ŻOB)

and other Resistance movements. Chilling and unmissable. 🕐 *30 min. Ul.Pomorska 2* ☎ *012-633-14-14. Free admission. May–Oct Tues–Sat, 2nd Sun of the month 10am–5.30pm. Nov–Apr Tues, Thurs–Sat, 2nd Sun of the month 9am–4pm, Wed 9am–5pm. All trams to Pl.Inwalidów.*

❷ ★ Army Museum. Surrounded by abandoned buildings gap-toothed with broken windows, Krakow's main military museum is in dire need of an overhaul. Its contents, filling a long hallway and a main room on the first floor, are certainly worthy of interest, the corridor displays relating to the Warsaw Uprising, the rest given over to the struggles of the 1930s and 1940s. Maps, medals, newspapers, gattling guns and sundry equipment tell of

Maps, medals and flags on display at the Army Museum.

the campaigns for Polish independence—so many with fatal consequences. There's not much documentation in English but the wealth of material more than makes up for it. Mention must be made of war-time leader Major Henryk 'Hubal' Dobrzański (1897–1940) whose heroic achievements are outlined in detail. ⏰ *30 min. Ul. Wita Stwosza 12* ☎ *012-430-33-63. Admission 5zł. Tues–Fri 11am–5pm. All trams to Dworzec Główny.*

3 Szpitalna 38. The lurid Midgard Music Club may seem an unlikely stop on any tour of war-time Krakow—but this venue was once the Cyganeria Café. A favorite meeting place for Nazi officers, it was busy with drink and chatter the night before Christmas Eve in 1942 when a bomb planted by the Jewish Fighting Organization killed 11 men and wounded a dozen others. Reprisals were swift—within three months the Nazis had liquidated the Ghetto, massacring many in the process. A plaque marks the blast site. ⏰ *10 min. All trams to Dworzec Główny.*

4 ★★ Old Synagogue. Krakow's oldest synagogue is one of two branches of the History of Krakow Museum dealing with Judaism. Outside a monument marks where 30 Poles were shot by the Nazis in 1943. Inside, a detailed exhibition covering the life, culture and rituals of local Jewry is complemented by a display upstairs of photographs, posters and documents relating to the Nazi occupation. The other synagogues of Kazimierz, the heart of the Jewish community decimated in the 1940s, have been gradually renovated. For further evidence of what happened then, you must cross the river from Kazimierz to Podgórze. (See Special Interest Tours: Jewish Krakow, p 27.) ⏰ *1 hr. Szeroka 24.* ☎ *012-422-09-62. www.mhk.pl.*

Plac Bohaterów Getta.

Last entry 30 min before closing. Mon 10am–2pm; Tues–Sun 9am–5pm. Admission 7zł/5zł. Free Mon. Trams 3, 9, 11, 13, 24: Wawrzyńca.

5 ★★ Plac Bohaterów Getta/ Pharmacy Under the Eagle. An open square crossed by trams and groups of tourists on the Schindler trail, the former Plac Zgody was where Jews were rounded up before deportation to the camps, and massacred on two dreadful days in March 1943. Seventy 70 chairs, an installation by Piotr Lewicki and Kazimierz Łatak dot the square, representing the furniture Jews were forced to abandon before being sent to the death camps. In the far corner stands Tadeusz Pankiewicz's Pharmacy Under the Eagle, converted to a branch of the History of Krakow Museum. Under brave Pankiewicz, the pharmacy became a resource and meeting place for Jews seeking to survive the Nazi occupation. Photographs, film and documentation record the Ghetto years in these three rooms—post-war letters of gratitude to Pankiewicz from around the world are framed and displayed.

Remnant of the Ghetto Wall.

🕐 *30 min. 18 Plac Bohaterów Getta* ☎ *012-656-56-25. Admission 5zł adults, 4zł students. Free Mon. Apr–Oct Mon 10am–2pm, Tues–Sun 9.30am–5pm. Nov–Mar Mon 10am–2pm, Tues-Thurs, Sat 9am–4pm, Fri 10am–5pm. Closed first Tues of the month. Trams 9, 13, 24, 34: Pl.Boh,Getta.*

❻ Remnant of the Ghetto Wall. A plaque in Polish and Hebrew illustrates the suffering of the Ghetto inhabitants here, one of only two fragments of the original wall. Noticeable are the half-moon shapes of each section, similar in design to traditional Jewish gravestones. 🕐 *10 min. Lwowska 25-29. All trams to Limanowskiego.*

❼ Schindler Factory. Thanks to the success and longevity of Steven Spielberg's film, this is the most famous stop on the Schindler tour— and perhaps the most disappointing. The sign still reads 'Fabryka Oskara Schindlera—Emaila', referring to the factory the Sudeten German ran here, a working haven for Jews away from the death camps—

but around it, windows covered in polythene tell of a building in need of renovation. Entry is forbidden. One positive step has been the factory's use as a venue for cultural events, most recently for the Sacrum Profanum festival. 🕐 *10 min. Lipowa 4. Trams 9, 13, 24, 34: Pl.Boh,Getta.*

❽ Amon Göth's Villa. Close to the Dworcowa tram stop and a drive-in McDonald's, lie the war-time sites of Płaszów, the large Nazi forced labor camp. Up the quiet pathway of Heltmana, this stand-alone house, shabby but not abandoned, was the residency of Amon Göth, the sadistic commander of Płaszów. There is no sign or plaque, just an eerie atmosphere emanating from behind the net curtains. From here, Göth directed operations, shooting and beating random victims on a daily basis. Göth was hanged near here in 1946. 🕐 *10 min. W. Heltmana 22. All trams to Dworcowa.*

Plaszow Memorial.

Entrance to Auschwitz II Birkenau.

9 ★ **Płaszów.** Spread over a large area behind Amon Göth's villa is the Liban Quarry, where thousands were worked to their deaths. Signs advise visitors to step with reverence, across the hilly, overgrown patch of land to the fenced-in site, rundown machinery still visible. If you follow the path from Heltmana 40c, along from Göth's villa, you come to a cross on a plinth and, beyond it, two more plaques. Towering over them rises the massive, stark monument to Płaszów's victims, erected in 1964. Six arms and five lowered heads seem fixed in reverence, visible from the main road between Krakow and Wieliczka. ⏱ *20 min. All trams to Dworcowa.*

10 ★★★ **Auschwitz.** The horror of all horrors. The two death camps of Auschwitz, 90 minutes by bus or train from Krakow, epitomize the evil of the Nazi regime. Dedicated, knowledgeable guides await the tourist busloads arriving from Krakow—it's well worth being shown around on this one. At Auschwitz I, through the gates bearing the slogan 'Arbeit Macht Frei', the neat rows of wooden huts are filled with reminders of the dreadful events here—suitcases, hair, glasses, all belonged to someone who met a terrifying death after a near unbearable ordeal. One gas chamber remains. A short bus ride away, Auschwitz II Birkenau demonstrates the scale of the terror—stumps of the original huts stretch as far as the eye can see. This is where you'll find the rail line leading to the arched gateway, used so often to signify the hopelessness of Auschwitz. (See The Best Day Trips and Excursions: Auschwitz, p 149.) ⏱ *2 hr. Ul.Więzniów Oświęcim 20, Oświęcim* ☎ *033-844-80-00. Admission free— guided tours vary. Children under 12 advised not to enter. May–Oct Daily 8am–6pm. Nov–Apr Daily 8am–5pm. All buses, trains and minibuses to Oświęcim or by frequent guided tour from Krakow.*

Krakow **with Kids**

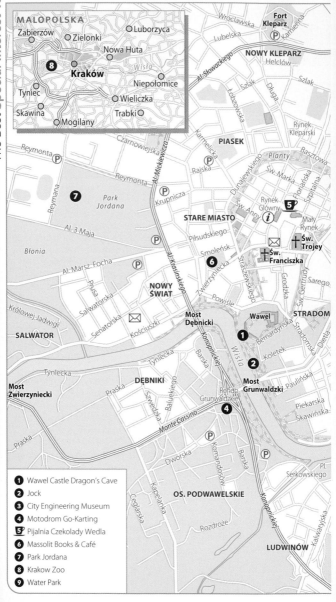

1 Wawel Castle Dragon's Cave
2 Jock
3 City Engineering Museum
4 Motodrom Go-Karting
5 Pijalnia Czekolady Wedla
6 Massolit Books & Café
7 Park Jordana
8 Krakow Zoo
9 Water Park

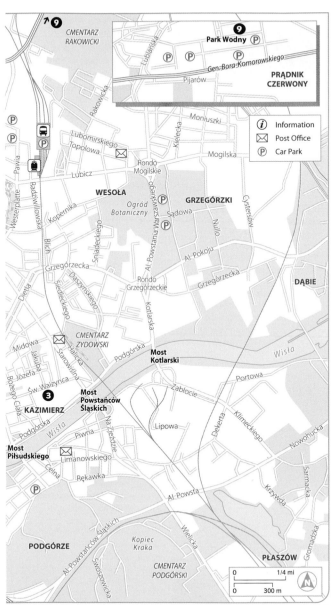

CMENTARZ RAKOWICKI

Park Wodny

PRĄDNIK CZERWONY

Gen. Bora-Komorowskiego

Pijarów

Lublańska

Moniuszki

Kielecka

Mogilska

(i) Information
⊠ Post Office
(P) Car Park

Lubomirskiego

Topolowa

Rakowicka

Rondo Mogilskie

Lubicz

WESOŁA

Pawia

Radziwiłłowska

Westerplatte

Kopernika

GRZEGÓRZKI

Ogród Botaniczny

Sądowa

Cystersów

Mogilska

Al. Powstania Warszawskiego

Nullo

Śniadeckiego

Daszyńskiego

Blich

Grzegórzecka

Al. Pokoju

Rondo Grzegórzeckie

Grzegórzecka

DĄBIE

Dietla

Siedleckiego

Kotlarska

CMENTARZ ŻYDOWSKI

Podgórska

Most Kotlarski

Wisła

Midowa

Halicka

Starowiślna

Jakuba

Józefa

Bożego Ciała

Św. Wawrzyńca

Portowa

Zabłocie

Klimeckiego

KAZIMIERZ

Most Powstańców Śląskich

Dekerta

Nowohucka

Podgórska

Wisła

Piwna

Na Zjeździe

Lipowa

Most Piłsudskiego

⊠

Limanowskiego

Celna

Rękawka

Sarmacka

Al. Powsta

Krzywda

Gromadzka

PODGÓRZE

Al. Powstańców Śląskich

Swoszowicka

Kopiec Kraka

Wielicka

PŁASZÓW

CMENTARZ PODGÓRSKI

0   1/4 mi
0   300 m

Safe, compact, car-light, central Krakow is one of Europe's easiest main cities to get around—no overcrowded subway trains or bustling five-abreast boulevards here. Nearly all bars, cafés and restaurant—not to mention locals—are child-friendly, too. But for hands-on entertainment, you may have to cast your net wide. The couple of interactive museums, the zoo, the Aqua Park and the main areas of green space are spread far apart, although city transport is good, cheap and equally easy to negotiate. The cycle-friendly green ring of Planty (see p 88) is another handy option for those confident on two wheels. Nearly all hotels are happy to accept kids as guests.

❶ ★★ Wawel Castle Dragon's Cave. Having dragged the kids round the seemingly endless historic rooms of Wawel Castle, the least you can do is treat them to a big thrill at the bottom of the Dragon's Cave. Linked to the legend of the dragon who resided here before being tricked into defeat by a wily local cobbler, the summer-only cave involves a downward hike through 160 metres of tunnels, chambers and corridors before you hit street level—and Bronisław Chromy's dragon statue scaring the pants off 4-year-olds with its regular fire-breathing antics. ⏱ *20 min.*

Wawel Castle's fire-breathing dragon.

Admission 3zł. Daily Apr–June, Sept–Oct 10am–5pm, July–Aug 10am–6pm. All trams to Wawel.

❷ ★ Jock. A sad story, this, so break it to them gently. Canine Jock ('Dżok') sat at this spot for months, near the Grunwald Roundabout, where his master had died of a heart attack in his car. Later befriended and fed by an old local, he was taken to the dog pound after her death, only to escape to seek his favorite spot again. Haring back to the waterfront site, Jock was hit by a train and killed. Heartbroken local dog lovers clubbed together to commission this statue, another Chromy creation. ⏱ *10 min. Bulwar Czerwieński. Trams 18, 19, 22: Orzeszkowej.*

❸ ★★ City Engineering Museum. It's well worth you beating a path through deepest Kazimierz to reach this rare interactive museum, spread out around an old tram depot. First make a beeline for the Fun and Science section, where feats of engineering are explained by letting kids build their own bridges, pull levers, press buttons and generally make things sparkle, crackle and bubble. The transport section—old trams and classic Polish-made cars through the ages—might appeal to vehicle-obsessed boys or Dads who haven't grown up

Classic Polish made cars at the City Engineering Museum.

yet. 🕐 *1hr. Ul.św.Wawrzyńca 15* ☎ *012-421-12-42. www.mimk.com.pl. Admission 6.50zł/4.50zł. June–Sept Tues–Wed, Fri–Sun 10am–4pm, Thurs 10am–6pm. Oct–May Tues–Sun 10am–4pm. Trams 9, 13, 24, 34: Wawrzyńca.*

④ ★★ Motodrom Go-Karting.

Moving from its Kazimierz base in 2007, the popular Motodrom has set up in the grounds of the disused behemoth Hotel Forum just over the river. Kids from 7 years old and up can whizz go-karts around the tyre-lined course, for varying prices and timed circuits from 8 minutes and up, Grand Prix flags and all. 🕐 *30 min. Ul.Konopnickiej* ☎ *012-421-48-65. Daily noon–10pm. Trams 18, 19, 22: Most Grunwaldzki. All buses to Rondo Grunwaldzkie.*

⑤ ★ Pijalnia Czekolady Wedla.

Wherever you're heading to or arriving from, you're bound to cross the main market square—and invariably pass this temple to chocolate and confectionery. Its grand surroundings befit a family tradition dating back 157 years. Wedel may have been taken over by UK's Cadbury in 1999, but they sure know how to present pralines, cakes and their trademark chocolates. This is a café too, so enjoy a sumptuous hot chocolate on a winter's afternoon while the kids get messy. *Rynek Główny 46.* ☎ *012-429-40-85. $$.*

⑥ ★ Massolit Books & Café.

Krakow's friendly English-language (mainly secondhand) bookshop has the laudable policy of holding children's book readings, in English, on Sundays. The age limit is 7. There's a café too, and plenty of kids' books to buy. 🕐 *1 hr. Ul.Felicijanek 4* ☎ *012-432-41-50. Free admission. Sun 11am. Trams 1, 2, 6: Jubilat.*

⑦ ★★ Park Jordana.

Krakow's main recreational park lies just west of the outer ring road, a short distance from the city centre. A fully equipped skate park installed in June 2008 complements the basketball and volleyball courts, slides, climbing frames and a lake for paddleboats. The park borders the expansive open common of Błonia, the domain of joggers, kite-flyers and dog walkers. 🕐 *2 hr. Aleja 3 Maja. Apr–Oct Daily 6am–10pm. Nov–Mar Daily 6am–8pm. Trams 15, 18: Park Jordana n/z.*

Boating lake at Park Jordana.

8 ★★ **Krakow Zoo.** Set in the middle of Las Wolski woods (see p 94), at the terminus of the 134 bus route from the Hotel Cracovia, Krakow's zoo has been in business for 80 years. Its global reputation as a breeding zoo is well earned— snow leopards, Andean condors, wild cats and lynxes have all been raised here in captivity. Local species get a good look in, boar, bison and alike. Mammals are given reasonable space—although some suffer from the bitter Polish winter. A snack bar by the main entrance overlooks the elephant enclosure. ⏱ *2 hr. Las Wolski* ☎ *012-425-35-51. Admission 14zł/7zł. Daily Summer 9am–7pm. Spring, Autumn 9am–6pm. Winter 9am–3pm. Bus 134: Zoo.*

9 ★★★ **Water Park.** Well worth the trek 5km north-east of town, Krakow's Park Wodny is superbly equipped, able to deliver a whole afternoon of fun. Pipes and slides include the world's longest Salamander shute, nearly 100 m of twists and turns for those 12 and above; a climbing wall where the water safely catches anyone who falls; a paddling pool with a fairytale castle for toddlers; eight jacuzzis; plus a lane pool and sauna for the grown-ups. ⏱ *2 hr. Ul.Dobrego Pasterza 126.* ☎ *012-616-31-90. Daily 8am–10pm. All buses to Dobrego Pasterza.* ●

Old **Town**

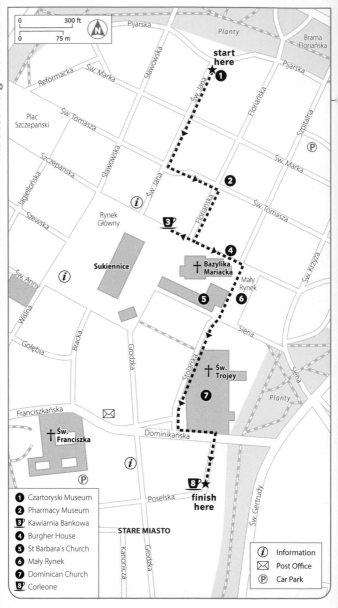

0	300 ft
0	75 m

Pijarska

Planty

Brama
Floriańska

start
here **1**

Św. Marka

Reformacka

Św. Marka

Pijarska

Floriańska

Słowowska

Św. Jana

Szpitalna

Plac
Szczepański

Św. Tomasza

Szczepańska

Jagiellońska

Słowowska

Św. Jana

2

Floriańska

Św. Tomasza

(i)

Szewska

Rynek
Główny

3 ☕

Floriańska

4

Św. Krzyża

Św. Anny

(i)

Sukiennice

✝ **Bazylika
Mariacka**

5

Mały
Rynek

6

Wiślna

Grodzka

Bracka

Gołębia

Siena

Siena

Stolarska

✝ Św.
Trojey

7

Planty

Franciszkańska

✉

✝ Św.
Franciszka

Dominikańska

(i)

8 ★
finish
here

(P)

Poselska

Św. Gertrudy

STARE MIASTO

Kanonicza

Grodzka

1 Czartoryski Museum
2 Pharmacy Museum
3 Kawiarnia Bankowa
4 Burgher House
5 St Barbara's Church
6 Mały Rynek
7 Dominican Church
8 Corleone

(i)	Information
✉	Post Office
(P)	Car Park

Krakow's Old Town offers relaxed tourism at its best. Easily walkable, with churches, shops and museums at almost every turn, the streets of the Stare Miasto surrounding the main market square provide no must-see but plenty to captivate the casual visitor. Don't worry about a map—the grid-pattern of well signposted streets is easy to negotiate, with a bagel seller or café to hand each time you step out of any church or historic attraction. START: **All trams to Barbican.**

① ★★★ **Czartoryski Museum.**
A cornucopia of random European treasures awaits at one of Krakow's most endearing museums. For a modest entrance fee of 10zł (free on Thursdays), you are treated to one of only three Da Vinci oil paintings in the world, *Lady with an Ermine*; a Rembrandt landscape; assorted worthy Spanish, Venetian and Flemish pieces, and any number of sabres, porcelain figures, medals and uniforms, as well as the assorted personal artifacts of Napoleon, Captain Cook and Frederick the Great. All is set over three floors, in a drawing-room atmosphere the Princess Izabela Czartoryska would have appreciated. Noble collector, a friend of Benjamin Franklin, Voltaire and Rousseau, the princess founded Poland's first

museum, the war booty and heirlooms forming the bulk of what you see here today. In those days, it was not considered manly to spend time collecting things. Originally housed at a purpose-built house at the Czartoryski family pile at Puławy, this collection of unique valuables had to be relocated to Paris before the political situation in Galicia calmed down in the later 1800s. Pick up a useful English-language audio guide unless you can negotiate the French or Polish documentation. ⏱ *1 1/2 hr. Św.Jana 19* ☎ *012-422-55-66. Admission 10zł adults, 5zł students and youths, free Thurs. May–Oct Tues, Thurs 10am–4pm, Wed, Fri, Sat 10am–7pm, Sun 10am–3pm. Nov–Apr Tues, Thurs, Sat–Sun 10am–3.30pm, Wed, Fri 10am–6pm.*

Czartoryski Museum.

MUZEUM
XX. CZARTORYSKICH

Burgher House, once home to the Hippolits family.

❷ ★ kids Pharmacy Museum.

Often overlooked despite its central location, this quirky attraction is full of surprises. One of the most voluminous of its kind the Pharmacy Museum fills five floors of a splendid 15th-century building, each done out to look like an apothecary from a particular century or, in the case of the basement and loft, an underground laboratory and herb-drying room respectively. Furniture, chests, cupboards and vessels are original, many taken from monasteries across Poland. The result feels authentic and close to how people lived down the centuries—more than many museums can muster with glassed-in cases of items and illustrations. 🕐 1 hr. Floriańska 25 ☎ 012-421-92-79. Admission 6zł adults, 3zł students. Tues noon–6.30pm. Wed–Sun 10am–2.30pm.

❸ Kawiarnia Bankowa.

On the Floriańska corner of the main market square, this terrace café is a handy pit stop for those exploring the north-east side of the Old Town. Renovated in 1998, with an interior dating back to the First World War, the Bankowa offers breakfasts and snacks along with the usual range of coffees and drinks. Rynek Główny 47 ☎ 012-429-56-77. $$.

❹ ★ kids Burgher House.

The Hippolits family lived in this grand townhouse at the turn of the 16th and 17th-centuries. The house, somewhat older, has been converted into a museum to illustrate the lives and pleasures of those who lived in Krakow at the time. Up a shiny wooden staircase, you are led through a series of rooms, each filled with furniture and objects relating to daily life at the time—the grandfather clock and bed-warmer in the bedroom, the keyboard in the music room, the visiting cards in the hallway.

St Barbara's Church on Maly Rynek square.

People watch from a café on Maly Rynek.

Documentation is in the form of laminated cards in English and Polish. So close to the main square you can hear the bugle player on the hour from St Mary's, the Burgher House provides a quiet and welcome distraction from the daily life of 21st century Krakow. ⏲ *45 min. Pl.Mariacki 3* ☎ *012-422-42-19. www.mhk.pl. Admission 6zł adults, 4zł students. Free Wed. May–Oct Wed–Sun 10am–5.30pm. Nov–Apr Wed, Fri–Sun 9am–4pm, Thurs noon–7pm. Closed 2nd Sun of the month.*

❺ St Barbara's Church. Generally only open for mass, St Barbara's was built around the same time as St Mary's diagonally opposite, reputedly with leftover bricks. Its façade is Gothic in appearance, with figures from the workshop of Veit Stoss (of St Mary's altar fame) at the entrance. Worth a quiet stroll around the outside. ⏲ *10 min. Maly Rynek* ☎ *012-428-15-00.*

❻ ★ Maly Rynek. The smaller (but not younger) of the two adjoining market squares in the heart of Krakow feels calm after the tourist mayhem of Rynek Główny. Used from medieval times as a meat market, the Maly Rynek rid itself of traders after the Second World wWar. The grand surrounds of

symmetrical townhouses and the sides of St Mary's and St Barbara's churches lend the Maly Rynek a dignified atmosphere—best enjoyed from one of the café terraces. ⏲ *10 min.*

❼ ★ Dominican Church. Standing at the gateway to the cluster of churches set between the main market square and Wawel, the Dominican Church is a late 19th-century rebuild of the 13th-century Gothic original. Many of the ornate chapels survived, most notably the Myszkowski, with busts of the family lining the dome. Of all the churches in Krakow, the Dominican attracts the most faithful congregation—mass here really is a thing to behold. ⏲ *30 min. Stolarska 12.* ☎ *012-423-16-13. Daily 8am–8pm.*

❽ Corleone. A standard but reliable Italian eaterie, happy to provide tasty favorites to weary sightseers at the end of a hard morning's work. Corleone currently offers lunchtime specials on weekdays—risotto is the recommended choice. Excellent selection of wines, too, augmented by Tuscan labels, a feature of Thursday wine-and-music evenings. *Poselska 19* ☎ *012-429-51-26. $$.*

University Quarter

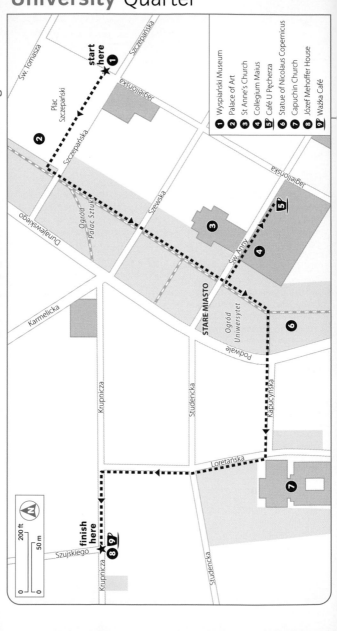

1 Wyspiański Museum
2 Palace of Art
3 St Anne's Church
4 Collegium Maius
5 Café U Pęcherza
6 Statue of Nicolaus Copernicus
7 Capuchin Church
8 Józef Mehoffer House
9 Ważka Café

start here 1

Św. Tomasza
Szczepańska
Plac Szczepański
Szczepańska
Jagiellońska
Jagiellońska
Dunajewskiego
Ogród Pałac Sztuki
Pałac Sztuki
Karmelicka
Szewska
STARE MIASTO
Ogród Uniwersytet
Św. Anny
Podwale
Kapucyńska
Krupnicza
Studencka
Loretańska
Studencka
Szujskiego
Krupnicza

finish here

8 9

200 ft
50 m

The venerable buildings of the Jagiellonian University dot cobbled streets, creating a tranquil, erudite atmosphere. The oldest, geared to tourists, is the Collegium Maius, where Krakow's most celebrated pupil, Nicolaus Copernicus (1473–1543), studied in the 1490s. A guide takes you around the 15th-century building, pointing out rare treasures including the oldest surviving globe to depict the Americas. Some 45,000 students enroll at 15 faculties—the University Quarter is as vibrant now as it was 500 years ago. **START: All trams to Teatr Bagatela.**

1 ★★ Wyspiański Museum.
The life and achievements of Stanisław Wyspiański, 19th century architect, art nouveau artist, poet and playwright, are celebrated at this renovated attraction. Two floors of paintings, plans, designs and models fill several small rooms—you'll find yourself overwhelmed at the range of Wyspiański's work. Self-portraits abound, plus studies of Wyspiański's contemporaries, including Józef Mehoffer in his studio. Theater sets and translated versions of Wyspiański's play *The Wedding* illustrate his literary output. Pride of place goes to a model of his revamped Wawel, 'Acropolis'. Rooms look out onto an ivy-clad courtyard, decorated with a house-sized copy of one of the artist's friezes. ⏱ *1 hr. Ul.Szczepańska 11* ☎ *012-422-70-21. Admission 8zł adults, 4zł students and youths, free*

Wyspiański Museum – home of artist, poet and playwright.

St Anne's, also known as the University Church.

Sun. May–Sept Tues–Fri 10am–6pm, Sat–Sun 10am–3.30pm. Oct–Apr Tues–Fri 11am–6pm, Sat–Sun 10am–3.30pm.

2 Palace of Art. The Secessionist Palace of Art, opened in 1901 belongs to the Friends of the Fine Arts organization. Busts of 19th-century Polish artists adorn Franciszek Mączyński's imaginative façade, designed to represent Doubt, Pain and Despair, through which every artist must travel. You can make out Wyspiański and Matejko, among others. ⏱ *15 min. Pl.Szczepański 4* ☎ *012-422-66-16.*

3 St Anne's Church.. Also known as the University Church—famous students and professors are represented, including Copernicus—baroque St Anne's was Gothic

but rebuilt in sumptuous style by Tylman van Gameren (1632–1706) in the late 1600s. The plasterwork and altars were the work of Baltasare Fontana—as you walk around the airy nave, it's hard to tell which pillars are real and which painted. To the right of the main entrance stands the shrine of St John of Kęty, also by Fontana, the remains of the former professor held up by figures representing four University faculties. ⏰ *15 min. Św. Anny 11* ☎ *012-422-53-18. Daily 9am–noon, 4pm–7pm.*

④ ★★★ kids Collegium Maius. Accessed by tour only—book your place on the next English-language one taking place that day—the first-floor University Museum contains remarkable treasures whose significance is entertainingly described by your guide. The 30 minutes fly by as you are shown lecture rooms and ceremonial halls, taking in a copper globe from the early 1500s with the Americas depicted for the first time; an astrolabe from Arabia dated 1054, and astronomical instruments from when Copernicus studied here in the 1490s. In the cramped

The church of the Capuchin friars.

Copernicus Room, your guide will point out discs, globes and instruments he would have used. Sadly, much of the paperwork is facsimile—the Swedes took the original Copernicus collection, kept today at the Uppsala University Library. Your visit, culminates with the ornate Aula where graduation ceremonies still take place. Text over its Renaissance portal reads: '*Plus Ratio Quam Vis*'—'Let Reason Prevail Over Strength'. A further hour-long tour takes in the permanent art collection (with pieces by Rembrandt and Rubens) a child-friendly interactive exhibition runs on occasional mornings. ⏰ *40 min. Ul.Jagiellońska 15* ☎ *012-422-05-49. Admission by tour only. 12zł adults, 6zł students. Free Tues Apr–Sept. Apr–Oct Mon, Wed, Fri 10am–2.20pm Tues, Thurs 10am–5.20pm, Sat 10am–1.20pm. Nov–Mar Mon–Fri 10am–2.20pm, Sat 10am–1.20pm.*

⑤ Café U Pęcherza. In the basement of the Collegium Maius, this labyrinthine café displays the Kashary archaeological dig near Odessa. Students chat casually over coffee, cakes and snacks beneath pictures of their professors unearthing Greek treasures. *Ul.Jagiellońska 15* ☎ *012-422-05-49. $.*

⑥ Statue of Nicolaus Copernicus. Outside the Collegium Novum on the edge of the Planty Krakow's most famous student is in a reflective mood, a primitive astronomical instrument to hand. The plinth refers to his year of study here being 1491. Behind stands the main University building, where concerts are given in the Aula Magna lecture hall. A plaque marks the professors sent to concentration camps in 1939. ⏰ *10 min.*

7 **kids** **Capuchin Church.** The church of the Capuchin friars reflects the simplicity of their Order—the real architectural treasure here is the Loreto Chapel, built outside in the early 1700s, two decades after the friars first arrived. Connected to the church by cloister, the chapel makes this brief diversion worthwhile with its statue of the Madonna within a striking altar. At Christmas, a mechanical nativity scene uses characters from Polish history and folklore. ⏱ *20 min. Loretańska 11* ☎ *012-422-48-03. Daily 9.30am-7pm. All trams to Teatr Bagatela.*

Statue of Nicolaus Copernicus.

The pretty garden and café at Jósef Mehoffer House.

8 ★ **Józef Mehoffer House.** A great find, this, partly because of its artistic treasures, partly because of the fin-de-siècle family atmosphere of this house-cum-museum, and partly because of the lovely café and garden. Artist and designer Mehoffer, a key member of the Młoda Polska artistic movement of the late 19th century, bought the house in 1932. It belonged to the grandmother of his great contemporary, Stanisław Wyspiański, born under its roof in 1869. Walking through the various family rooms, their design and furnishings arranged by Mehoffer himself, you see how little has changed here– a room of 50 Japanese woodblock prints looks as it did in a 1938 photograph. The house was converted to a museum by Józef's son Zbigniew in 1969, on the centenary of his father's birth. ⏱ *40 min. Ul.Krupnicza 26* ☎ *012-292-64-48. Admission 6zł adults, 4zł students. Free Sun. Tues–Sat 10am–6pm. Sun 10am–2pm. All trams to Teatr Bagatela.*

9 **Ważka Café.** With seats and tables facing the pretty garden of the Józef Mehoffer House, the 'Dragonfly' is a cut above most museum cafés. Dishes include goulash and soljanka soups, pierogi and beef stroganoff or you could opt for a slice of cake and a fruit tea. The ideal end to any attraction-laden day. *Ul.Krupnicza 26* ☎ *012-292-64-48. $.*

Wawel

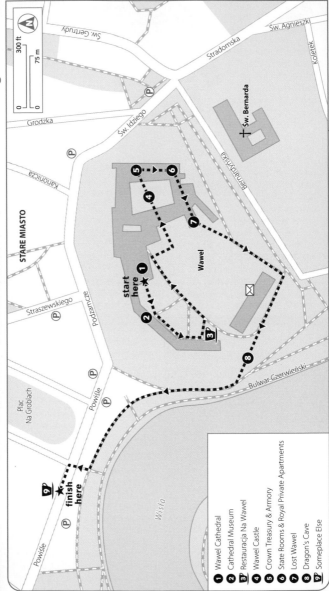

STARE MIASTO

Wawel

start here

finish here

Plac Na Groblach

Wisła

Św. Gertrudy
Stradomska
Św. Agnieszki
Koletek
Grodzka
Św. Idziego
Św. Bernarda
Kanonicza
Bernardyńska
Straszewskiego
Podzamcze
Powiśle
Bulwar Czerwieński
Powiśle

300 ft
75 m

❶ Wawel Cathedral
❷ Cathedral Museum
❸ Restauracja Na Wawel
❹ Wawel Castle
❺ Crown Treasury & Armory
❻ State Rooms & Royal Private Apartments
❼ Lost Wawel
❽ Dragon's Cave
❾ Someplace Else

Wawel is Krakow's Westminster Abbey, Notre-Dame and Vatican. As you climb its steep hill, a wall naming the donors who paid for Wawel's renovation a century ago, the sense of history is palpable. This is where Polish kings were crowned, where Polish monarchs, poets and generals lie buried, and where trophies from historic Polish battles were presented. At the main gate, a digital ticker records sales of timed tickets up to the day's limit—be in line in time and you'll get in. Tour groups are also admitted, a stress-free but pricier option. Restricted visitors allow easy access, even with kids—you won't wait long for a snack at two outlets or use the toilets. START: **All trams to Wawel.**

① ★★★ kids **Wawel Cathedral.** Poland's most sacred building is a visual assault. Buying your ticket opposite the Cathedral, you enter the three-aisled nave crammed with treasures and lined with bright chapels and ornate tombs. Crypts await,below. Following the arrows your eye picks out the most striking elements: the Zygmunt Chapel, on the right-hand side, is the Renaissance at its most exquisite; in the middle, the tomb of King Jan III Sobieski (1629–1696), hero of the Battle of Vienna, is baroque; and, near it, the tomb of King Jan Olbracht (1459–1501) is late Gothic. On the left-hand side is the entrance to the

Royal Crypt and, further along, is the Zygmunt Tower. The former involves a shuffle around tombs grouped by dynasty, although those of military heroes and poets give light relief. For the tower, climb the narrow, steep staircase for views of Krakow. The clapper of the Zygmunt Bell, 2 m in diameter, is only used for special occasions—reach up to touch it with your left hand for luck. ⏱ *1hr 30min. Wawel 3* ☎ *012-429-33-27. www.wawel.krakow.pl. Last entry 30 min before closing. Admission 10zł/5zł. May–Sept Mon–Sat 9am–5pm, Sun 12.30pm–5pm. Oct–Apr Mon–Sat 9am–4pm, Sun 12.30pm–4pm.*

Poland's most sacred building—Wawel Cathedral.

② ★ **Cathedral Museum.** Turn immediately right as you come out of the Cathedral and you arrive at a modest building and a small square front garden. This is the Cathedral Museum, opened by Archbishop Karl Wojtyła (1920–2005) in 1978 before becoming Pope. Over two floors, you'll find robes and regalia of sundry Polish kings—the brightest being the coronation robe of Stanisław August Poniatowski (1732–1798), dated 1764—and oddities such as four slabs from the tenth-century St Gereon's Church. Much of the top floor is given over to paraphernalia pertaining to John Paul II, either as Pope or Archbishop of Krakow. 🕓 *40min. Wawel 3* ☎ *012-429-33-27. www.wawel.krakow.pl. Admission included with Wawel Cathedral ticket. May–Sept Mon–Sat 9am–5pm. Oct–Apr Mon–Sat 9am–4pm.*

③ **Restauracja Na Wawel.** The only full-blown restaurant in the Wawel complex, this one offers hefty meat dishes with all the trimmings, three kinds of fish, four soups and a good selection of blini. Not cheap, but the expansive terrace looking over Krakow more than compensates. There's a cheaper separate snack bar. *Wzgórze Wawelskie 9* ☎ *012-421-19-15. $$.*

④ ★★★ **kids** **Wawel Castle.** A short walk from the Cathedral leads to an arcaded Renaissance courtyard, surrounded on three sides by a fine three-story Italianate building crammed with historic goodies. Modest queues form by the doorways of two main museums: the State Rooms and Royal Private Apartments; and the Crown Treasury and Armory, both requiring tickets from the main kiosk. Round the corner, within the outer

courtyard gardens centerpiecing the Wawel complex, is the Lost Wawel exhibition. The people making strange movements in the northwest corner of the inner courtyard are reacting to the energy said to resonate from the black stone of the former St Gereon's Church behind the wall. *Wawel Hill* ☎ *012-422-51-55 ex 219. www.wawel-krakow.pl. Daily 6am–dusk.*

⑤ ★ **kids** **Crown Treasury & Armory.** The lesser of the two inner courtyard museums will impress the boys with its many swords, cannons, crossbows, muskets and spiky things on chains. As for the Treasury, the assortment of medals, coins and goblets includes an 11th-century chalice belonging to the Tyniec abbots. 🕓 *40 min. Admission 14–15zł/7–8zł. Free Nov–Mar Sun. Apr–Oct Tues–Fri 9.30am–5pm, Sat–Sun 11am–6pm. Nov–Mar Tues–Sun 9.30am–4pm.*

⑥ ★★ **kids** **State Rooms & Royal Private Apartments.** Here, top-floor State Rooms involve a lengthy but enjoyable walk through numerous interconnecting doorways, leading to elaborately decorated spaces. Look out for the

Wawel Castle.

The Renaissance courtyard at Wawel Castle.

Hans Dürer scenes in the Tournament Room and Flemish tapestries in the Planet, Eagle and Envoys' Rooms, where 30 carved heads on the ceiling are what the kids will be raving about. You access the Royal Private Apartments by guided tour, hence the higher ticket price—but the Flemish tapestries, Meissen porcelain and rich furnishings make it worthwhile. Don't miss the 14th-century Gothic Hen's Foot tower, Renaissance paintings, a fireplace from 1600 and a view of Krakow from the windows. ⏲ *40 min. Admission 19–20zł/14–15zł. Apr–Oct Tues–Fri 9.30am–5pm, Sat–Sun 11am–6pm. Nov–Mar Tues–Sat 10am–4pm.*

7 ★★ **kids** **Lost Wawel.** A millennium of finds from Wawel Hill are displayed around a descending series of spiral walkways—visitors stop to gawp at kitchenware, leather shoes and paving tiles used here down the centuries. The foundations of the 10th—century Rotunda that once stood here, and models of St Gerleon's Church and Wawel in its various stages, also draw interest. A film show of

historic treasures plays by the entrance. ⏲ *40 min. Admission 7zł/4zł. Apr–Oct Free Mon. Nov–Mar Free Sun. Apr–Oct Mon 9.30am–1pm. Tues–Fri 9.30am–5pm, Sat–Sun 11am–6pm. Nov–Mar Tues–Sun 10am–4pm.*

8 ★★ **kids** **Dragon's Cave.** Every kid's favorite attraction at Wawel. Linked with the legend of a dragon overcome by a wily shoemaker, this summer-only amusement takes you down 160 m of tunnels, chambers and corridors until you arrive at the Vistula embankment—and Bronisław Chromy's dragon statue breathing out great sparks of fire ⏲ *20 min. Admission 3zł. Daily Apr–June, Sept–Oct 10am–5pm, July–Aug 10am–6pm.*

9 **Someplace Else.** The Sheraton Hotel's terrace sports bar, near the exit of the Dragon's Cave, offers the family easy Tex-Mex choices from noon on. Live music makes a longer stay worthwhile for the grown-ups. *Powiśle 7* ☎ *012-662-16-70. $$.*

Kazimierz

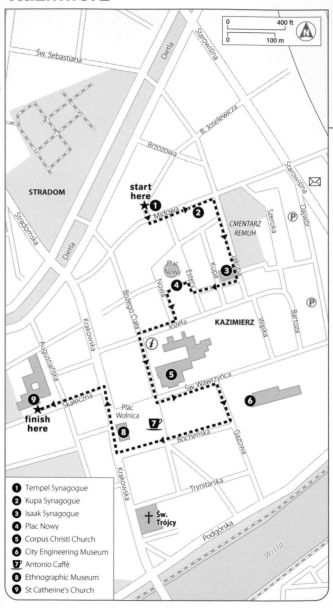

STRADOM

start here
★ ❶

CMENTARZ REMUH

Plac Nowy

❷

❸

❹

KAZIMIERZ

❺

❻

Plac Wolnica

❾
finish here

❽ ❼

❶ Tempel Synagogue
❷ Kupa Synagogue
❸ Isaak Synagogue
❹ Plac Nowy
❺ Corpus Christi Church
❻ City Engineering Museum
❼ Antonio Caffè
❽ Ethnographic Museum
❾ St Catherine's Church

✝ Św. Trójcy

Kazimierz has sprung to life of late. Where there were once only desultory remnants of the rich Jewish culture thriving here before the Second World War, today a new Kazimierz has emerged. Krakow's most happening bar hub contains contemporary, cosmopolitan restaurants, major outlets at a recently opened mall and a 10-screen cinema complex. Most of all, the long dormant Jewish culture is vibrant again, with regular cultural events and a major annual festival. The Christian churches and unusual museums clustered in this compact district echo Kazimierz as it once was: historic, bohemian and multicultural. START: **All trams to Krakowska/Dietla.**

1 ★★ **Tempel Synagogue.** Of Kazimierz's half-dozen synagogues, the first you find as you cross over at the Dietla/Krakowska crossroads is perhaps the most attractive—and controversial. Built outside the original 17th-century ghetto walls, the Tempel was also known as the Progressive Synagogue for the inclusive nature of its services. Built in the 1860s by Jews who had been assimilated into the local culture, the Tempel features three dozen stained-glass windows, with inscriptions in Polish and Hebrew—traditionalists were horrified! Today the Tempel is best visited during one its regular chamber concerts. It also hosts the opening of June's Jewish Culture Festival. ⏱ *20min. Miodowa 24* ☎ *012-429-57-35. Admission 5zł/2zł. Mon–Fri, Sun 9am–4pm.*

2 ★ **Kupa Synagogue.** The recent substantial renovation of this 350-year-old synagogue comes after five decades of neglect. Biblical scenes and images of Israel now embellish the ceiling, signs of the Zodiac in the women's gallery and the depictions of Noah backdrop concerts and exhibitions regularly held here. General admission is free, making the Kupa a pleasant and easy diversion on any local wander. ⏱ *15 min. Miodowa 27. Mon–Fri, Sun 9am–6pm.*

3 ★ **Isaak Synagogue.** The biggest of Kazimierz's synagogues has also benefited from recent major renovation. The 17th- and 18th-century murals are now restored and visitors are greeted with a video loop of original

Tempel, also known as the Progressive Synagogue.

Kupa Synagogue.

newsreel films shot around Kazimierz in less peaceful times, one of general street life in the 1930s, the other of Nazi round- ups. 🕐 *20min. Kupa 18 ☎ 012-430-55-77. Admission 7zł/4zł. Mon–Fri, Sun 9am–7pm.*

4 ★ **Plac Nowy.** The square at the heart of Kazimierz sums up its history and contemporary revival perfectly. Known by locals as Jewish Square, 'New Square' is

Corpus Christi Church, founded by Kazimierz the Great.

centrepieced by a round market building which Jews used as a poultry slaughterhouse before the war. Now it is ringed by little hatches serving toasted sandwiches in long, half-baguette form, wielded by barhoppers as they flit from venue to venue around the café-choked square. Plac Nowy still operates as a market: produce in the week and secondhand clothes on Sundays.

5 ★★ **Corpus Christi Church.** As you walk south from Plac Nowy, you are entering the old Christian part. Its tower rising 70 m over the Kazimierz skyline, the church founded by Kazimierz the Great (1310–1370) in the 1300s is a mixture of styles reflecting its patchwork history. Raided by Swedish, Russian and Austrian troops, Corpus Christi offers unusual but worthy features in various architectural styles. Walking round the spacious grounds, used as a graveyard in the 16th century, you come across a roofed, caged-in model of Christ in the Garden of Gethsemane, an image that stays with you as you enter the Gothic portal. Features of the three-aisled interior include a boat-shaped pulpit, mermaids, oars, fishing nets, and, in the north aisle, the tomb of Florentine architet Bartolomeo Berecci (1480–1537).

Responsible for many of Wawel's Renaissance touches, Berecci died in odd circumstances in the market square in 1537. ⏱ *20min. Bożego Ciała 25. Mon–Sat 9am–7pm.*

⑥ ★★ kids City Engineering Museum.

More entertaining than its name suggests, this museum set in a former tram depot should keep most kids occupied for an hour or so. Few museums in town offer a hands-on approach, so the Fun and Science section's interactive take on science and engineering is welcome. Children can construct bridges and make models spark, move and wobble. The transport section concentrates on Polish models, such as a Polski Fiat car from 1936, weird post-war prototypes (look out for the back-to-front one from 1957) and classic local makes from the 1960s. ⏱ *1hr. Ul.św.Wawrzyńca 15 ☎ 012-421-12-42. www.mimk.com.pl. Admission 6.50zł/4.50zł. June–Sept Tues–Wed, Fri–Sun 10am–4pm, Thurs 10am–6pm. Oct–May Tues–Sun 10am–4pm.*

Motorbikes at the City Engineering Museum.

⑦ Antonio Caffè.

An easy and pleasant option on a main square , this shiny red café offers Italian standards, cakes, sorbets and quality appetizers. Chic decorative touches keep the clientele selective. *Wolnica 13 ☎ 012-430-59-99. $.*

⑧ ★★ kids Ethnographic Museum.

Set in Kazimierz Town Hall, a striking building dating back to the 1500s, the Ethnographic Museum is thorough, imaginative and surprisingly entertaining. Starting on the ground floor with five life-size reproductions of peasant houses from specific villages in Poland—note the tiny beds, bizarre snowshoes and cheese presses—the permanent exhibition moves upstairs to the extensive section concentrating on the life cycle in rural Poland in the 19th and early 20th centuries. Birth, toys, pastimes, school, farm life, work, military service, church, weddings, political life, institutions, newspapers, music and family celebrations are exhaustively illustrated with a wealth of material (artifacts, film, interviews) with documentation also given in English. The second floor is given over to popular art, pottery and textiles. ⏱ *1hr. Pl. Wolnica 1 ☎ 012-430-55-63. www. mek.krakow.pl. Admission 8zł/5zł. Tues–Wed, Fri–Sat 11am–7pm, Thurs 11am–9pm, Sun 11am–3pm.*

⑨ ★ St Catherine's Church.

One of Krakow's most beautiful Gothic churches stands on Kazimierz's far western edge, towards the river. Founded by Kazimierz the Great in the 1300s, it contains murals from that era, in the cloisters, but many of the other historic features within have been lost in earthquakes and invasions. Look out for the baroque altar and Gothic vestibule. ⏱ *30 min. Ul. Augustiańska 7 ☎ 012-430-62-42. Mon–Fri 10am–3pm, Sat 10am–2pm, Sun 1.30pm–5pm.*

Podgórze

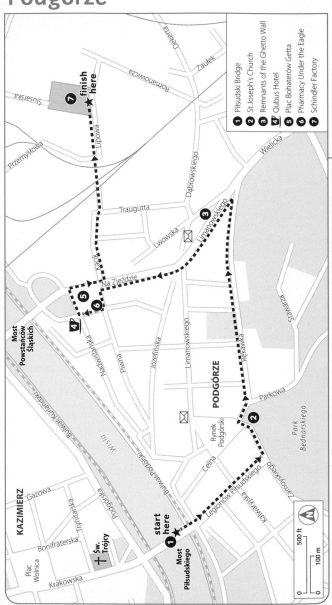

1 Piłsudski Bridge
2 St Joseph's Church
3 Remnants of the Ghetto Wall
4 Qubus Hotel
5 Plac Bohaterów Getta
6 Pharmacy Under the Eagle
7 Schindler Factory

finish
here

7

Śląska
Przemysłowa
Lipowa
Romanowicza
Dekerta
Zaułek

Traugutta

Lwowska
Limanowskiego
Kącik
Na Zjeżdzie

Dąbrowskiego

Wielicka

5
6
4

Nadwiślańska
Piwna
Józefińska
Limanowskiego
Rękawka
Parkowa

Stawarza

Most
Powstańców
Śląskich

PODGÓRZE

2

Park
Bednarskiego

KAZIMIERZ

Bulwar Kurlandzki
Bulwar Podolski
Wisła
Podgórska
Trynitarska
Gazowa

Plac
Wolnica

Bonifraterska

Krakowska

Św.
Trójcy

Rynek
Podgórski

Celna

Kalwaryjska
Legionów Piłsudskiego
Zamoyskiego

start
here

1

Most
Piłsudskiego

N

500 ft
100 m
0
0

Immediately facing Kazimierz over the Vistula, Podgórze was the location of the war-time Jewish Ghetto. Although inevitably linked with the terrible events of the 1940s, Podgórze is enjoying a major revival. Bars and restaurants that would have comfortably rubbed shoulders with the fashionable spots of Kazimierz three years ago have been set up this side of the river. This ever-growing cluster of chic, bohemian destinations set amid sites many would recognize from the Steven Spielberg film *Schindler's List*—remnants of the Ghetto, the Płaszów workcamp and the original factory itself. It all makes for an eerie mix, tourists following the Schindler tour while locals hang out in trendy bars on the edge of the old Ghetto. START: **Trams 3, 6, 8, 10: Korona.**

1 Piłsudski Bridge. The most dramatic of the bridges over the Vistula was opened in 1933. Three cast-iron arches rise criss-crossed over the river, allowing views of historic Wawel and the new businesses of Podgórze on each side. Built to ease the pressure off the nearby Habsburg Podgórski Bridge, since demolished, the Piłsudski Bridge now seems in constant motion, the regular rattle of trams and traffic vibrating under the feet of pedestrians as they cross on the outer footpaths. The Podgórze side is ideal for a waterside stroll, back towards town. *See p 86.*

2 ★ St Joseph's Church. Look towards Podgórze from anywhere in the city and this spire dominates the skyline—prolific church architect Jan Sas-Zubrzycki (1860–1935) was hoping to copy the landmark effect that the spire of St Mary's has on the main market square of the Old Town. Opened in 1909, when the Habsburgs still controlled this rival side of the river, the large neo-Gothic St Joseph's church towers over Podgórze's own main market square, but is somewhat underwhelming once you enter—take a walk around its recently renovated exterior for a better impression. *Rynek Podgórski.*

Piłsudski Bridge on the Vistula.

St Joseph's, built by prolificchurch architect Jan Sas-Zubrzycki.

③ ★ Remnants of the Ghetto Wall.
Of the original 3-m high wall created in March 1941 to pen in Krakow's Jews, only two fragments remain. On this one on Lwowska, a plaque in Polish and Hebrew speaks of their suffering. The top of the wall was created in a running, half-moon pattern—an easily identifiable visual association with the shape of traditional Jewish gravestones. It's not much to see but what there is gives a clear idea of how the neighbourhood was brutally divided during the Nazi occupation. ⏱ *10 min. Lwowska 25-29.* *See p 36.*

④ Qubus Hotel.
If anything strikes the most contrast between the remnants of war-time tragedy and 21st-century Podgórze, it's this glitzy business and leisure hotel, opened in 2006. Take a break from a morning on the Schindler trail with coffee, cakes or open sandwiches at the Barracuda lobby bar. The After Work piano bar and Mile Stone jazz club provide swish drinks and entertainment for those arriving from early evening. *Nadwiślańka 6* ☎ *012-374-51-00. $$.*

⑤ ★ Plac Bohaterów Getta.
The former Plac Zgody, renamed 'Heroes of the Ghetto', was the site of the regular round-ups and appalling Nazi massacre of Jews in March 1943. Today it is dotted with

Plac Bohaterów Getta.

Pharmacy Under the Eagle, now a museum documenting the ghetto years.

70 chairs, the contemporary installation by Piotr Lewicki and Kazimierz Łatak harking back to the time when Jews had to discard their furniture before being sent to the death camps. As always, it is the everyday that brings the weight of history into focus. The façades of new shops and businesses do little to diminish your imagination as your eyes gaze over the stark, open square. 🕐 *15 min. Trams 9, 13, 24, 34: Pl.Boh.Getta. See p 35.*

6 ★★ Pharmacy Under the Eagle. Converted to a museum in 1983, Tadeusz Pankiewicz's original pharmacy was a resource and meeting place for Jews during the Nazi occupation. Photographs, film and documentation record the Ghetto years in these three rooms—the sense of recent, tragic history is palpable. Note the wooden cabinet from the original apothecary still set behind the ticket desk by the main door as you go in. A portrait of Pankiewicz is displayed in the back room, surrounded by letters of thanks written by Holocaust survivors from around the world. 🕐 *30 min. Plac Bohaterów Getta 18*

☎ *012-656-56-25. Admission 5zł adults, 4zł students. Free Mondays. Apr–Oct Mon 10am–2pm, Tues–Sun 9.30am–5pm. Nov–Mar Mon 10am–2pm, Tues–Thurs, Sat 9am–4pm, Fri 10am–5pm. Closed first Tues of the month. Trams 9, 13, 24, 34: Pl.Boh.Getta. See p 35.*

7 Schindler Factory. Although closed, its windows covered over with polythene and bin bags, this landmark on the Schindler trail continues to attract a steady stream of tourists. The main entrance, bearing the sign 'Fabryka Oskara Schindlera—Emaila', otherwise looks as you would have seen in Steven Spielberg's film. Occasionally used for exhibitions and concerts, the Schindler Factory (and all its connotations) come into their own for festivals such as September's Sacrum Profanum, set in former industrial spaces. A performance of music by Karlheinz Stockhausen in 2008 created a particular resonance in this most atmospheric of historic settings. Stockhausen's radical sounds were inspired by his traumatic war-time experiences. 🕐 *10 min. Lipowa 4.*

Nowa **Huta**

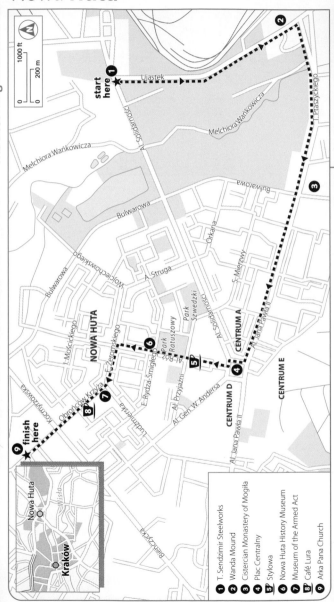

1000 ft
200 m
0
0

start here
① Ujastek
②
③
Melchiora Wańkowicza
T. Ptaszyckiego
Melchiora Wańkowicza
Bulwarowa
Bulwarowa
Wojciechowskiego
A. Struga
Orkana
S. Mierzwy
NOWA HUTA
I. Mościckiego
E. Żeromskiego
Al. Solidarności
Park Ratuszowy
Park Szwedzki
Al. Jana Pawła II
CENTRUM A
④
⑤
⑥
Obrońców Krzyża
Ludźmierska
Al. Przyjaźni
Al. Gen. W. Andersa
CENTRUM D
CENTRUM E
⑧
⑦
finish here
⑨
Kocmyrzowska
Mista
Nowa Huta
Kraków
Bieńczycka

① T. Sendzimir Steelworks
② Wanda Mound
③ Cistercian Monastery of Mogiła
④ Plac Centralny
⑤ Stylowa
⑥ Nowa Huta History Museum
⑦ Museum of the Armed Act
⑧ Café Lura
⑨ Arka Pana Church

There is nowhere quite like Nowa Huta, a living, full-scale museum. Arriving from 21st-century Krakow, you enter a brave new world laid out by post-war Communist planners, wide, arrow-straight avenues radiating from an open central square. One, named after the Solidarity movement whose local demonstrators sheltered in the nearby labyrinthine housing blocks, leads to the vast steel-works complex around which Nowa Huta was built. The plant still produces half of Poland's steel—little seems to have changed since the 1950s, the main attraction for making the 20-minute tram ride from town. Many shops, bars and places of entertainment look exactly as they did decades ago. By contrast, the leafy pre-war village of Mogiła a short walk away is an easy, bucolic getaway. **START: Tram 4 to Kombinat.**

1 ★ T. Sendzimir Steelworks. Renamed after the pioneering Polish metal engineer, the former Lenin Steelworks are vast. Tours (by appointment) to the 1,000-hectare complex are organized on the internal bus system, negotiating roads running for scores of kilometers. Passes in advance can be arranged at the main office by the factory gates—unusually, the management is happy for people to visit, even though the plant is still a working one, employing some 10,000 locals. For most, a photo at the main gates is enough, the factory name spelled out in suitably huge, striking letters. ⏱ *10 min. Tram 4: Kombinat.*

2 ★★ kids Wanda Mound. A 10-minute walk or one stop on the 21 tram takes you from recent history to Krakow's ancient roots. Tucked away through the bushes by the factory fence, this prehistoric man-made hillock is said to be the burial place of Princess Wanda, daughter of the city's mythical founder, the dragon-slayer Krak. An easy climb brings you to the top, marked by a white eagle on a plinth, with a view of the factory complex below. ⏱ *15 min. Tram 21: Kopiec Wandy.*

The former Lenin Steelworks, now named after T. Sendzimir the Polish engineer.

Nowa Huta by Trabant

You walk into the tiny, dark lobby of the Hotel Floryan at the far end of Florianka in the Old Town. The receptionist rings a number and hands you the receiver. 'This is Crazy Mike,' says the voice. 'When do you want us to come?' Booking a tour with Crazy Guides, organizers of personalized trips to Nowa Huta in original Trabant cars, is not unlike the event itself—random, unpredictable and bags of fun. At the appointed time, the crazy guide himself—Victor, Bartek or Mike—arrives at your hotel and gestures to the transport of Commie delight, customized in striking black and red, and embellished with a five-pointed star. You squeeze into the vehicle, one of millions produced in East Germany until 1991, and as you rattle towards Nowa Huta, your guide begins his own history of the area—the riots, the crackdown, the characters. His stories continue as you're taken around Nowa Huta, meeting locals as you do so. The brainchild of Michał 'Mike' Ostrowski, a hotel receptionist who started taking guests around in his Polski Fiat, Crazy Guides has expanded from the basic two-hour tour (119zł) of Nowa Huta's main sights to include lunch at an original milk bar, visits to his mother's authentically retro apartment, evenings at a 1980s' disco and even airport pick-ups by Trabbie. A huge success since launching in 2004, Crazy Guides (www.crazyguides.com) also runs trips to a traditional farm and four-hour visits to Krakow behind the scenes.

❸ ★ **Cistercian Monastery of Mogiła.** Another 15-minute walk or a couple of tram stops and you're in the historic village of Mogiła, site of this monastery and church founded in the 13th century. Entering the grand gates, you cross the peaceful, well-kept gardens, centerpieced by a statue of St Bernard of Clairvaux, 12th-century abbot and key figure of the Cistercian order. Take the trouble to walk around the Abbey Church, open to visitors—Renaissance murals and an intricate altar of the Madonna and Child are housed in the three-aisled basilica, embellished with blue stained-glass windows. Across the road, the wooden 15th-century Church of St Bartholomew only opens for mass but visitors may walk around its tranquil grounds. ⏱ *15 min. Klasztorna. Trams 15, 20: Klasztorna.*

❹ ★ **Plac Centralny.** All roads (and tramlines) lead to Nowa Huta's main square, grand, spacious and hexagonal. Controversially named after Ronald Reagan (although still referred to on maps—and by locals—as Plac Centralny), the square is a classic example of Communist planning. The most eminent architects of the day were brought in to landscape an urban design of Renaissance façades and Socialist-Realist housing—four housing estates stand behind the Italianate archways. Arriving from cramped, tourist-swamped Krakow, Plac Centralny feels open and airy, elongated views stretching along its five radial avenues as far as the horizon.

5 ★ **Stylowa.** Opened in 1956 'Style' retains its once-classy-now-retro interior, along with a pleasant beer terrace, recently branded by a local beer company. Come here and you've definitely been to Nowa Huta. Seen-it-all waitresses in traditional garb serve cheap Polish drinks and standard dishes, with a heavy slice of irony. Breakfasts include herring and smoked salmon; lunches (tripe, chops, steaks) and can be accompanied by the wonderfully named cucumber in cream: mizeria ze śmietaną. *Os.Centrum 3. $.*

6 ★ **Nowa Huta History Museum.** Up focal Aleja Róż from Plac Centralny, this local information office and museum in-one is a useful stop on any tour of Nowa Huta. Staff seem delighted by the arrival of any foreign visitor, breaking out copies of the English-language 'Nowa Huta District Guide' and map, and talking visitors through whichever temporary exhibition happens to be staged in the modest space alongside. All have a local theme, so

All the roads in Nowa Huta lead to Plac Centralny.

expect posters and black-and-white photographs of heroic workers with backdrops of a Socialist paradise. ⏲ *30 min. Os.Sloneczne 16.* ☎ *012-425-97-75. www.mhk.pl/oddzialy_ nhuta.php. May-Oct Tues–Sat, 2nd Sun of the month 9.30am–5pm. Nov–Apr Tues, Thurs-Sat, 2nd Sun of the month 9am–4pm. Wed 10am–5pm. Admission 4zł/3zł. Wed Free.*

Stalin's IS-2 tank outside the Museum of the Armed Act.

Arka Pana Church.

7 Museum of the Armed Act. A bizarre one, this. Round the corner from the Nowa Huta History Museum stands one of Stalin's IS-2 tanks, one that saw action in the Second World War. Behind it, renovated and reopened in September 2008, is an exhibition detailing heroic action taken by locals during the conflict. Documents, uniforms, weapons and medals are displayed across one floor, with one section set aside for the war-time letters of Jan Anioła, first director of the steelworks. ⏲ *15 min. Os.Górali 23* ☎ *012-644-35-17. Tues–Fri 10am–3pm.*

8 Café Lura. Attached to the landmark People's Theatre, this terrace café serves snacks and cakes to locals by day, and pre-show drinks to theatergoers by night. Some of Krakow's most challenging and exciting productions have been staged here since 1955—particularly during the times of authoritarian repression. *Os.Teatralni 24* ☎ *012-680-21-12. $.*

9 ★★ Arka Pana Church. A fitting end to any tour of Nowa Huta is this quite remarkable church, as astonishing in its construction as it is in appearance. Over the course of 10 years, with no financial or logistical help from the authorities, locals built their church by hand, bringing in two million stones bag by bag from the countryside. Work was even stalled by the discovery of 5,000 war-time bombs and shells. Wojciech Pietrzyk's ark-shaped design stands out now as it did upon the church's consecration in 1977, as does Bronisław Chromy's bronze statue of Christ, positioned as if about to fly over the congregation. Set in the tabernacle is a small piece of rutile mineral brought back from the moon by Apollo 11. ⏲ *30 min. Obrońców Krzyża.1* ☎ *012-644-54-34. Lower level Daily 6am–6pm. Upper level Closed during mass. Trams 1, 5: Teatr Ludowy.* ●

Shopping Best Bets

Best **Wacky Antiques**
★★★ Galeria Osobliwości,
Ul.Sławkowska 16 (p 73)

Best **Hip Designer Clothing**
★★★ Punkt, *Ul.Sławkowska 12
(p 76)*

Best **Krakow Souvenirs**
★★ Galeria Dom Polski, *Pl.Mariacki
3 (p 78)*

Best **Gourmet Foods**
★★★ Likus Concept Store, *Rynek
Główny, 13 (p 82)*

Best **Vodka Selection**
★★★ Szambelan, *Ul.Gołębie
(p 82).*

Best **Dip into Old-World
Krakow**
★★ Księgarnia Hetmańska, *Rynek
Główny 17 (p 74)*

Best **Mall for Kids**
Galeria Kazimierz, *Ul.Podgorska 34
(p 79)*

Best **Secondhand Books In
English**
★★★ Massolit Books & Café,
Ul.Felicjanek 4 (p 74)

Best **One-Stop Shopping**
Galeria Krakowska, *Ul.Pawia 5
(p 80)*

Best **Urban Gear**
★ UFO/Underground, *Ul.Floriańska
13;* ★★ Tatuum, *Rynek Główny 37
(p 77)*

Best **Range of International
Books and Magazines**
★★ Empik, *Rynek Główny 5 (p 73)*

Best **Polish Chocolates**
★★ Wawel, *Rynek Główny 33
(p 82);* ★★★ Wedel, *Rynek Główny
46 (p 82)*

Best Polish Chocolates: Wawel.

Best **Amber Jewelry**
★★★ Boruni World of Amber, *Sukiennice, Rynek Główny 1/3 (p 79);*
★★★ Ora Gallery, *Ul.Św.Anny 3/1a
(p 79)*

Best **Postcards and Posters**
★★ Galeria Plakatu, *Ul.Stolarska
8-10 (p 78);* ★★ Galeria Autorska
Andrzeja Mleczki, *,Ul.Św.Jana 14
(p 78)*

Best **Contemporary Menswear**
★★ Vistula, *Rynek Główny 13
(p 77)*

Best **Contemporary
Ladieswear**
★★★ Hexeline, *Rynek Główny 11
(p 76)*

Best **Shoes With Style**
★★ Nunc, *Ul.Rakowicka 11 (p 76)*

Central Shopping

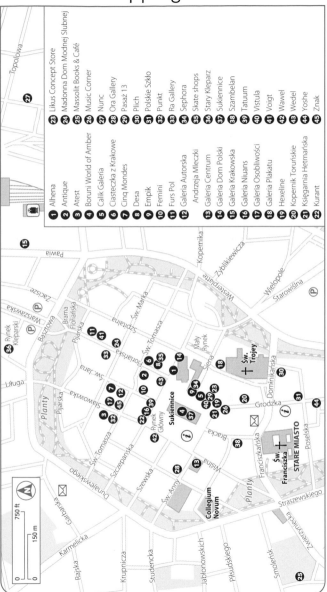

23 Likus Concept Store
24 Madonna Dom Modnej Ślubnej
25 Massolit Books & Café
26 Music Corner
27 Nunc
28 Ora Gallery
29 Pasaż 13
30 Plich
31 Polskie Szkło
32 Punkt
33 Ra Gallery
34 Sephora
35 Skate shops
36 Stary Kleparz
37 Sukiennice
38 Szambelan
39 Tatuum
40 Vistula
41 Voigt
42 Wawel
43 Wedel
44 Yoshe
45 Znak

1 Alhena
2 Antique
3 Atest
4 Boruni World of Amber
5 Calik Galeria
6 Ciasteczka z Krakowe
7 Cinq Mondes
8 Desa
9 Empik
10 Femini
11 Furs Pol
12 Galeria Autorska Andrzeja Mleczki
13 Galeria Centrum
14 Galeria Dom Polski
15 Galeria Krakowska
16 Galeria Niuans
17 Galeria Osobliwości
18 Galeria Plakatu
19 Hexeline
20 Kopernik Toruńskie
21 Księgarnia Hetmańska
22 Kurant

Kazimierz Shopping

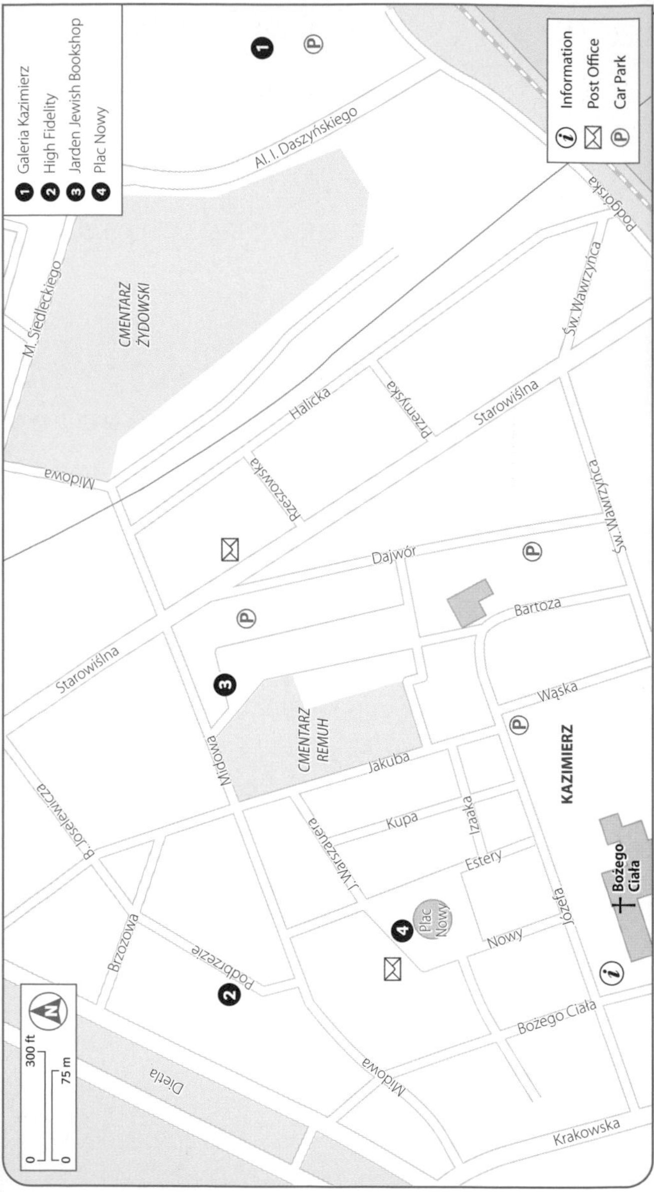

1 Galeria Kazimierz
2 High Fidelity
3 Jarden Jewish Bookshop
4 Plac Nowy

i Information
⊠ Post Office
Ⓟ Car Park

Al. I. Daszyńskiego

Podgórska

M. Siedleckiego

CMENTARZ
ŻYDOWSKI

Św. Wawrzyńca

Halicka

Przemyska

Starowiślna

Rzeszowska

Miodowa

⊠

Dajwór

Ⓟ

Bartoza

Ⓟ

Starowiślna

Wąska

3

Miodowa

CMENTARZ
REMUH

Jakuba

Ⓟ

KAZIMIERZ

B. Joselewicza

Kupa

Izaaka

Estery

Józefa

Brzozowa

Podbrzezie

Nowy

Bożego
Ciała

2

⊠

i

Bożego Ciała

Dietla

Miodowa

Krakowska

300 ft
75 m
0
0

Krakow Shopping **A to Z**

Antiques & Art
★ **Antique** OLD TOWN   Exquisite pieces of art, silverware, porcelain, jewelry and furniture are ranged around this historic townhouse, in business as an antique boutique since 1991. The store is particularly strong on 19th¯ and 20th-century paintings, and Empire-style furniture. *Ul.Św.Tomasza 19.* ☎ *012-421-79-44. AE, MC, V. Map p 71.*

★ **Atest** OLD TOWN   A reliable antiques store where historic items of furniture, jewelry and cutlery are bought, sold and assessed by experienced staff who have been working here for time immemorial. They are well versed in dealing with foreign customers and can advise on the legalities of exporting pre-war Polish antiques. *Ul.Sławkowska 14.* ☎ *012-421-95-19. AE, MC, V. Map p 71.*

★★ **Desa** OLD TOWN   In business for more than half a century, this chain of atmospheric antiques salons and auction houses holds regular sales. At this chief branch near the main square, you feel welcome to browse the paintings, jewelry, ornaments, cabinets and sundry artifacts spread over two floors. *Ul.Floriańska 13.* ☎ *012-421-89-87. www.desa.art.pl. AE, MC, V. Map p 71.*

★★★ **Galeria Osobliwości** OLD TOWN   Otherwise known as the Este, this marvelous Gallery of Curiosities was founded by Zbylut and Katarzyna Grzywacz in 1992. During that time, a remarkable array of bizarre items have passed through the store—not only art, furniture and jewelry but minerals, fossils, African figurines, masks, even a number of didgeridoos. Well worth

Find curiosities at Galeria Osobliwosci.

a browse even if you're not thinking of buying anything. *Ul.Sławkowska 16.* ☎ *012-429-19-84. www.este. krakow.pl. AE, MC, V. Map p 71.*

Books, Press & Stationery
★★ **Empik** OLD TOWN   Hard to think that this contemporary, nationwide, multi-media print, film and music chain of superstores has been going for 60 years. Its largest Krakow branch right on the main market square, the former International Book and Press Club today sells the world's press from its crowded ground-floor space. As you ascend by lift or staircase, you'll find guides, children's books, maps, novels and manuals in English and Polish, plus CDs, DVDs and coffee-table photo albums for special occasions. There's a photo department too, and an internet café on the third

floor. *Ul.Rynek Główny 5.* ☎ *012-423-81-90. www.empik.com. AE, DC, MC, V. Map p 71.*

★ Jarden Jewish Bookshop

KAZIMIERZ   Hundreds of titles relating to Jewish life, history and culture are stocked here, many of them in English, right in the heart of Kazimierz. Recipe books, guides, local histories, novels and biographies are ranged in easy-to-find rows around the large space, as well as a significant number of volumes on Auschwitz—Jarden is the official Krakow outlet of the publishing house there. *Ul.Szeroka 2.* ☎ *012-421-71-66. www.jarden.pl. AE, DC, MC, V. Map p 72.*

★★ Księgarnia Hetmańska

OLD TOWN   A fabulous treasure trove, this, in the historic house of the same name. A window display of jigsaw puzzles, globes, pictorial maps and Krakow-related tomes drag you from the main square into a three-space store of mainly books and attractive souvenirs. Hardbacks and guides, many in English, are

Books and souvenirs at Ksiegarnia Hetmanska.

lined in the room on the left-hand side, mainstream and children's books on the right, with T-shirts, buttons and sundry knick-knacks in the corridor between them. *Ul.Rynek Główny 17.* ☎ *012-430-24-53. www.hetmanska.pl. AE, MC, V. Map p 71.*

★★★ Massolit Books & Café

NOWY ŚWIAT   This attractive emporium, tucked down a quiet backstreet, is not only Krakow's main purveyor of secondhand books in English but a great café, reading room, local resource and meeting place in one. The books are all neatly arranged and easy to find in a back room accessed through an entrance where coffee, cakes and topical magazines are available for your delectation. Stools, ladders and a friendly staff help you negotiate the towering shelves and signposted rows. Some of the presentation hardbacks are almost impossible to resist. Massolit also organizes regular readings, children's too, and its noticeboard in the hallway is a handy advertising service for longer term expats. *Ul.Felicjanek 4.* ☎ *012-432-41-50. www.massolit.com. AE, MC, V. Map p 71. See p 41.*

★ Znak OLD TOWN   This old-school bookstore is the outlet for an erudite organization that also produces its own literary monthly. A significant number of foreign titles is available here, many of them in English. *Ul.Sławkowska 1.* ☎ *012-422-45-48. AE, MC, V. Map p 71.*

China, Crystal & Ceramics

★★★ Alhena OLD TOWN   At a suitably prestigious address, this boutique carries some of the finest examples of local glass, crystal and silverware. Polish firms such as Gerlach, Krosno and Jasło are well represented, with items ranging from bowls and lamps to ladles and ashtrays. If you're looking for that special cut-glass vase, this is where to come. *Pl.Mariacki 1.* ☎ *012-421-54-96. www.alhena.pl. AE, MC, V. Map p 71.*

★ **Galeria Niuans** OLD TOWN   A wealth of beautiful objects for the everyday use in the home are on display in this tasteful boutique on the main market square. Items in china, silver, smoked glass and crystal come by way of Swedish firms Kosta Boda and Orrefors, Haviland from Limoges and Esteban from Paris. Galeria Niuans is also the major Polish outlet for French Baccarat crystal. You can find Millefiori scents and candles from Milan—but sadly nothing by Polish manufacturers. *Ul.Rynek Główny 39.* ☎ *012-429-54-46. www.galerianiuans.pl. AE, DC, MC, V. Map p 71.*

★ **Polskie Szkło** OLD TOWN   Ewa Adamczyk's store along the Royal Route stocks an attractive selection of cut-glass artifacts, vases, lights, bowls and glasses. All purchases are attractively wrapped and make for suitable presents. *Ul.Grodzka 36.* ☎ *012-422-57-39. MC, V. Map p 71.*

Cosmetics & Perfumes
★★ **Cinq Mondes** OLD TOWN This is the main outlet in Poland for Jean-Louis Poiroux's exotic treatments and cosmetics. Aroma therapies, products for spa and ayurvedic massages and any number of potions for beautifying the body from China, Japan and India are available, along with expert advice. These products and treatments are also used at the Farmona Business Hotel and Spa on the outskirts of the city. *Ul.Św.Jana 20.* ☎ *012-422-39-45. www.beautyboutique.pl. AE, DC, MC, V. Map p 71. See p 138.*

Cut-glass goods at Polskie Szkło.

★ **Sephora** OLD TOWN   Two outlets of the international French cosmetics chain are situated in Krakow city centre—this one and one at Floriańska 19. All the top global brands are here, most notably those of Helen Rubinstein, born in Krakow in 1870. You'll also find Sephora's own creams, fragrances, moisturizers and gift packs. *Rynek Główny 5.* ☎ *012-422-43-05. www.sephora.pl. AE, DC, MC, V. Map p 71.*

Fashion & Accessories
★★ **Femini** OLD TOWN   Local Krakow designer duo Monika Pietrzak-Szlęk and Katarzyna Wilk-Filipowicz creates some of Poland's most beautifully styled and patterned women's clothing—as displayed at London Fashion Weeks in recent years. Striking skirts, blouses and bridal wear are displayed at this boutique, also stocking items by the Warsaw Young Polish Designers' Foundation. *Ul.Św.Jana 5.* ☎ *012-429-19-83. www.femini.pl. AE, DC, MC, V. Map p 71.*

Furs Pol OLD TOWN   Fur coats, wraps and garments of all types are

Halina Zawadzka's fashion line at Hexeline.

stocked at this old-school store, here since the year dot on Floriańska. Ladies of a certain age serve clients with experienced aplomb in varnished wood surroundings. *Ul.Florianska 51.* ☎ *012-422-31-39. AE, DC, MC, V. Map p 71.*

★★★ **Hexeline** OLD TOWN Frequently cited in annual Polish 'entrepreneur of the year' lists, Halina Zawadzka has run this women's fashion brand since the 1980s. With another outlet in the Galeria Kazimierz and some 20 other Polish cities, plus Russia, Kazakhastan, the Ukraine and across central Europe, Hexeline is known for its seasonal collections displayed on the main market square. Superbly cut clothes in sought-after fabrics show modern style but classic influences. Zawadzka and her team are on the look-out for more landmark properties in town. *Rynek Główny 11.* ☎ *012-429-43-76. www.hexe.com.pl. AE, DC, MC, V. Map p 71.*

★ **Madonna Dom Modnej Slubnej** OLD TOWN This Viennese firm specializing in wedding dresses has had a base in Poland for three decades, with this branch in Krakow its main outlet. Madonna is the city's showcase for Spain's renowned designers Pronovias, and its San Patrick and La Sposa lines. Veils, necklaces, handbags and other accessories are also on show for you to choose the right appearance for the big day. Madonna has a smaller store in the Bielak Passage, off the main market square at number 9. *Ul.Florianska 39.* ☎ *012-422-24-00. www.madonna.pl. AE, DC, MC, V. Map p 71.*

★★ **Nunc** NEAR OLD TOWN Just east of the Old Town past the train station is an unlikely setting for the outlet of one of Krakow's—Poland's, in fact —most original designers. Krakow-born Dominika Nowak graduated at the Jagellonian University and in fashion at the Studio Bercot in Paris, and her hand-made shoes, clothes and accessories show the influences of both countries. Sold and presented at fashion shows around the world, Nowak's creations use natural materials, most notably animal hide—goat skin, cowhide, horse leather. This, her first boutique and concept store, opened in 2006, and presents her seasonal collections. *Ul.Rakowicka 11.* ☎ *0694-65-54-02. www.nunc fashion.com. AE, DC, MC, V. Map p 71.*

★★ **Plich** OLD TOWN As exclusive as it gets, Plich is renowned for creating individual pieces to order—original skirts, blouses and dresses sewn on request, with four-figure euro price tags attached to them. Considered to be a Polish trademark of style and distinction. *Ul.Dominikanska 3.* ☎ *012-430-19-22. AE, DC, MC, V. Map p 71.*

★★★ **Punkt** OLD TOWN Awarded the British Council's International Young Fashion Entrepreneur for 2008,

Monika Drożyńska is responsible for one of Krakow's most exciting and original stores. Vintage clothes recycled and completely remodeled (Drożyńska specializes in putting little ears on hooded tops), all-purpose handbags that can double up as a picnic blanket, Punkt is sassy and imaginative. Now opening a new store just along the street at number 24, Punkt is the most happening young brand in town. *Ul.Sławkowska 12.* ☎ *0511-56-25-26. www.punkt. sklep.pl. AE, DC, MC, V. Map p 71.*

★ **Skate shops UFO/Underground** OLD TOWN These two adjoining skate shops, set below the renowned auction house Desa, stock a bright range of urban streetwear—Etnies and dcshoecousa trainers, baseball caps, wallets, belts, bags, T-shirts—as well as boards and skates. *Ul.Florianska 13.* ☎ *012-422-54-35. MC, V. Map p 71.*

★★ **Tatuum** OLD TOWN With branches all over Poland and Eastern Europe (Prague, Budapest, St Petersburg), this domestic brand of casual and contemporary fashion for men and women is one of the country's best exports. Stark white walls bring out Tatuum's bright colors in urban and holiday wear at this branch, right on the main market square. *Rynek Główny 37.* ☎ *012-431-27-52. www.tatuum.pl. AE, DC, MC, V. Map p 71.*

★★ **Vistula** OLD TOWN With more than 50 outlets across the country, Krakow-based Vistula is one of Poland's most successful brands of menswear. Original chic, sharp suits and jackets come with each seasonal collection, vogueish looks for the young chap around town. With stores in most of the city's malls as well as this major showcase on the main market square, Vistula also carries the Lantier and Lettfield lines, and the more formal shirts of business partner Wólczanka. A made-to-measure service is also available for gentlemen of size. *Rynek Główny 13.* ☎ *012-617-02-64. www.vistula.com. pl. AE, DC, MC, V. Map p 71.*

★ **Voigt** OLD TOWN In business since the turn of the past century, and at this prestigious address for 80 years, the original firm of Helen Voigt today stocks the most contemporary glasses and shades in town—Ray-Ban, Police, Marc O'Polo, all the top brands. It can

Recycled and re-modelled vintage at Punkt.

Posters galore at Galeria Plakatu.

sort you out an eye test too. *Ul.Flori-anska 47.* ☎ *012-422-34-62.* *www.voigt-optyk.pl. AE, DC, MC, V.* *Map p 71.*

★ **Yoshe** OLD TOWN   Another strong local brand, Yoshe produces a select number of ladies' clothes, scarves, handbags and accessories each season. Trendy but accessible, classy but affordable, Yoshe's original pieces fill a gap in the market and provide an attractive, contemporary shop window right on the Royal Route. *Ul Grodzka 45.* ☎ *012-421-26-57. AE, DC, MC, V. Map 71.*

Gifts & Souvenirs

★★ **Calik Galeria** OLD TOWN   If you're visiting in December, call in to this main-square boutique for traditional and original Christmas ornaments. Trinkets in glass, wood and other materials can be beautifully wrapped and presented. Look out for characters in Polish folk costumes and the irrepressible Krakow dragon. *Rynek Główny 7.* ☎ *012-421-77-60. www.calik.pl. Map p 71.*

★★ **Galeria Autorska Andrzej Mleczki** OLD TOWN   If you're looking for something with a personal touch, then the much-loved works of revered cartoonist Andrzej Mleczko should be just the thing.

Posters, postcards, mugs and T-shirts feature the Polish equivalent of The Far Side. *Ul.Św.Jana 14.* ☎ *012- 421-71-04. http://mleczko. interia.pl. Map p 71.*

★★ **Galeria Dom Polski** OLD TOWN   The Polish Home Gallery, in the same building as the tourist information office, is a handy stop for items with a little more taste and character than the Sukiennice nearby. Ceramics, candles, animal-shaped objects for everyday use around the home, glassware and paintings are attractively set out for a good browse. *Pl.Mariacki 3.* ☎ *012- 431-16-77. www.galeriadp. com. AE, MC, V. Map p 71.*

★★ **Galeria Plakatu** OLD TOWN   An interesting store, this, stocking hundreds of local-language film, theater and circus posters, as well as the work of Poland's most famous exponents of the genre—Sebastian Kubica, Jan Sawka and Eugeniusz Get-Stankiewicz. Ask for a solid holder to keep them in if you're moving on backpacking. *Ul.Sto-larska 8-10.* ☎ *012-421-26-40.* *www.cracowpostergallery.com. AE, MC, V. Map p 71.*

★★★ **Sukiennice** OLD TOWN   The most prominent—and most picturesque—port of call for your gifts is the Cloth Hall, slap in the middle of the main market square. Stalls of leather goods, folky artifacts, hats, lace, woodcraft and sundry souvenirs line the historic hall thronging with tourists. There's nothing particularly exclusive, imaginative or original but it's a handy one-stop resource while doing a bit of sightseeing at the same time. *Rynek Główny. Map p 71.*

Jewelry & Amber
★★★ Boruni World of Amber
OLD TOWN   With 7 shops in Krakow city centre including this prominent one in the main square, this is one of the biggest local purveyors of amber. Necklaces, earrings, rings and assorted jewelry and trinkets—including sugar bowls, letter openers and chess pieces—have been intricately crafted with silver and gold to produce crafted artifacts redolent of any visit to Poland. *Sukiennice, Rynek Główny 1/3. ☎ 012-430-24-01. www.boruni.pl. AE, DC, MC, V. Map p 71.*

★★★ Ora Gallery OLD TOWN
Contemporary designs of amber and rare stones stand out at this jewelers, with necklaces, earrings, pendants and rings glittering beneath display cases. Not the cheapest boutique of its kind in the city but the quality is reliably good. *Ul.Św.Anny 3/1a. ☎ 012-426-89-20. www.galeria-ora.com. AE, DC, MC, V. Map p 71.*

★★ Ra Gallery OLD TOWN
Maria Radziszewska's imaginative creations of artistic jewelry in amber and silver are displayed and sold at two downtown venues, here on Floriańska and at Mikołajska 24 (012-423-26-27). *Ul.Floriańska 30. ☎ 012-431-16-83. AE, MC, V. Map p 71.*

Malls & Department Stores
★★ Galeria Centrum OLD TOWN
With the recent takeover by chic local menswear firm Vistula, there's a new style to this once Communist-era departments store on the corner of the main market square. GC is now strong on modern ladies' wear, lingerie and children's clothes (with many items produced here exclusively) as well as its traditional bent for textiles and international cosmetics. *Ul.Św.Anny 2. ☎ 012-422-98-22. www.galeriacentrum.pl. AE, DC, MC, V. Map p 71.*

★★★ Galeria Kazimierz KAZIMIERZ   Two floors of more than

Look for souvenirs at Sukiennice.

100 outlets (Lego, Swarovski, Timberland, Samsonite) are complemented by a modern multiplex cinema and the usual café and fast-food outlets. The kids can be entertained at various play areas. Special buses are laid on for shoppers from Planty and Wawel. *Ul.Podgorska 34.* ☎ *012-433-03-33. www.galeria kazimierz.pl. Map p 72.*

★★★ **Galeria Krakowska** NEAR OLD TOWN If anything reflects Krakow's recent transformation it is this vast, shiny, three-story mall opened by the train station in late 2006. Fashion gets most focus— more than a third of the 270 outlets sell clothes and accessories, with brands such as Zara, Versace, Pierre Cardin and Benetton. There are a dozen sports retailers (Puma, adidas, Nike) too. Some 25 outlets serving snacks and fast food keep the family fed and watered. *Ul.Pawia 5.* ☎ *012-428-99-00. www.galeria-krakowska.pl. Map p 71.*

★★★ **Pasaż 13** OLD TOWN Krakow's one-stop solution for everything chic, elite and boutique is this medieval basement lined with the likes of LFC, Vinoteka 13, Likus Concept Store and the upscale delicatessen Delikatesy 13. *Rynek Główny 13.* ☎ *012-617-02-27. www.pasaz13.pl. AE, DC, MC, V. Map p 71.*

Markets

★★ **Plac Nowy** KAZIMIERZ Centerpieced by the former Jewish poultry slaughterhouse of the Rotunda, this open square accommodates some 300 stalls selling fruit and vegetables, flowers, meat and dairy products. On Sunday mornings, the square is transformed into Krakow's main flea market. Neglected until the late 1990s, bar-lined Plac Nowy is now the most happening nightlife hub in the city – many locals spend their Sunday morning browsing the bric-a-brac before a relaxing drink and lunch at one of the many cafes. *Plac Nowy. Map p 72.*

★★★ **Stary Kleparz** NEAR OLD TOWN It's been here for centuries, this produce market just the other side of the Old Town ring road. Today some 70 stalls and outlets sell

Stary Kleparz for local food produce.

fruit and vegetables, flowers, meat, bread and cheese. Not to be confused with Nowy Kleparz, a more modern (and more expensive) marketplace at the far northern end of Ul.Długa. *Basztowa/Kryzwa.* ☎ *012-634-15-32. www.starykleparz.com. Map p 71.*

Music
★★★ **High Fidelity** KAZIMIERZ Krakow's best trove of secondhand records, CDs and books are stacked in fruit boxes in this intimate shop in a quiet Kazimierz side street. Great for finding obscure Polish 45s from the 1970s and '80s, handy as kitsch presents for friends back home. *Ul.Podbrzezie 6.* ☎ *0506-18-44-79. Map p 72.*

★★ **Kurant** OLD TOWN CDs and books are kept behind glass cases and on behind-the-counter wooden shelves at this old-school music store on the main square. There's a good selection of Polish folk and jazz CDs, as well as music and stories for children. *Rynek Główny 36.* ☎ *012-422-98-59. www.kurant. krakow.pl. MC, V. Map p 71.*

★★ **Music Corner** OLD TOWN The latest pop, rock, jazz, classical and DVD releases are stocked at this spacious, easy-to-use store on the main square. Also try Empik (p 73)

Old school music store Kurant.

for that recent film or album you're looking for. *Rynek Główny 13.* ☎ *012-421-82-53. www.musiccorner.pl. MC, V. Map p 71.*

Specialty Food & Drink
★ **Ciasteczka z Krakowe** OLD TOWN Delicate litte cakes, fruit teas, chocolate pralines and pretty presentation boxes of local sweet treats are all on offer here. *Ul.Św.Tomasza 21.* ☎ *012-423-22-27. www.ciasteczka-z-krakowe.pl. MC, V. Map p 71.*

Prime Shopping Zones

You'll find Krakow's finest boutiques for clothes, jewelry, souvenirs and up-market goods on focal **Rynek Główny** and the two main streets leading off it north and south, **Floriańska** and **Grodzka**. Nearly 300 retail outlets can be found at the **Galeria Krakowska**, just off Floriańska by the train station, with half as now open at the more modest **Galeria Kazimierz** in the district of the same name. For fresh produce, the age-old **Stary Kleparz** market is a short walk from the station too.

Likus Concept Store.

★★★ Kopernik Toruńskie Pierniki OLD TOWN Nearby

Toruń has a tradition of making gingerbread going back centuries. In its main Krakow outlet, you can pick up gingerbread in all kinds of shapes and coatings. Many are nicely packaged in boxes in designs (stars, planets) relating to Toruń's most famous son, Copernicus. *Ul.Grodzka 14.* ☎ *012-431-13-06. www.kopernik. com.pl. MC, V. Map p 71.*

★★★ Likus Concept Store OLD

TOWN Upmarket delights are stocked in this basement delicatessen in the Pasaż 13 centre—chocolates, spirits, sweets—mainly sourced from regional manufacturers. *Rynek Główny 13.* ☎ *012-617-02-50. AE, DC, MC, V. Map p 71.*

★★★ Szambelan OLD TOWN

The best selection of vodkas in town are found here, along with olive oils and sundry preserves. The bottles make ideal gifts—simply pick an attractive shape and have one of the knowledgeable staff here fill it with the concoction of your choice. *Ul.Gołębie 2.* ☎ *012-430-24-09. www.szambelan.com.pl. AE, DC, MC, V. Map p 71.*

★★ Wawel OLD TOWN All kinds

of chocolate products are sold at this prominent store—wafers, candies, pralines, cocoa and boxes for gifts and souvenirs. *Rynek Główny 33.* ☎ *012-423-12-43. www.wawel. com.pl. AE, DC, MC, V. Map p 71.*

★★★ Wedel OLD TOWN One of

Poland's best loved chocolatiers, in business for 150 years, runs this store and elegant café on the main square. Wedel, taken over by Cadbury Schweppes in 1999, is best known for its wonderful pralines—honey, amaretto, rum—sold individually or in presentation boxes. *Rynek Główny 46.* ☎ *012-429-40-85. www.wedelpijalnie.pl. AE, DC, MC, V. Map p 71.* ●

Waterfront

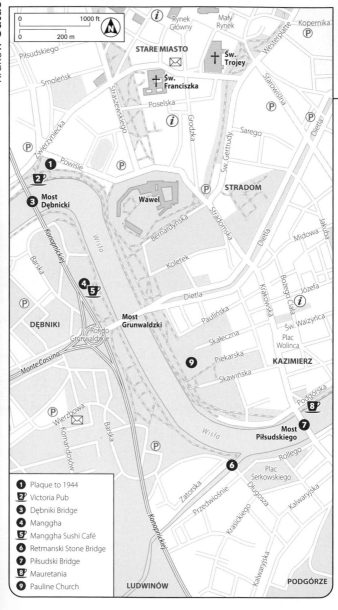

1. Plaque to 1944
2. Victoria Pub
3. Dębniki Bridge
4. Manggha
5. Manggha Sushi Café
6. Retmanski Stone Bridge
7. Piłsudski Bridge
8. Mauretania
9. Pauline Church

The Vistula waterfront is sadly underused around Krakow city centre. Couples canoodling on the grass slopes beneath Wawel, a couple of floating bars and the odd boat tour are the only immediately obvious activities. But investigate a little and you'll find contemporary Japanese art, a top-quality sushi bar, memories of a tragic, failed war-time assassination, an old stone bridge and a church linked with a thousand-year-old legend. And you'll be rewarded an afternoon's riverside stroll away from all the tourist crowds.

1 Plaque to the Underground Heroes of 1944. As you walk towards the Jubilat shopping centre from the Sheraton Hotel, cast your eyes away from the river to find this plaque topped by a Polish eagle. It marks the spot where members of the Polish Underground attempted to assassinate SS general Wilhelm Koppe in July 1944, a few days

Plaque to the Underground Heroes of 1944.

before the attempt on Hitler's life. Having survived, Koppe later ordered the execution of all Polish prisoners before the advancing Soviets. After going underground, Koppe ran a chocolate factory in Bonn and died a free man in 1975. The plaque names the five would-be assassins, giving each of their nicknames. ⏱ *10 min. Powiśle/Zwierzyniecka.*

2 Victoria Pub. Just below the Dębnicki Bridge in summer, two boat bars are set up side by side. This is the first one you come to, with two decks of bar space, the outer upper one giving a pleasant breeze off the river as you sip your draught Okocim. There are modest bar snacks too, and a fridge full of Magnum ice-creams. *Powiśle/ Dębnicki Bridge. $.*

3 Dębnicki Bridge. Compared to Prague or Budapest, Krakow's bridges are prosaic. This one was at least designed to be low enough so as not to obscure the beautiful view of Wawel from the opposite bank. When it was opened in 1952, the bridge connected the south-west of the city with the residential district of Dębniki. It still does but it also carries traffic from Slovakia and Zakopane away from the Old Town and north towards Kielce and Warsaw—it's busy. Crossing its 157-m span, your feet

Take a stroll by the Vistula waterfront.

Manggha sushi café and terrace.

are constantly rattling until you reach the eerie calm of the south bank. ⏲ *10 min.*

④ ★★★ **Manggha.** The Museum of Japanese Art and Technology is one of Krakow's most underrated treasures, located over the river from Wawel. Many of the items were bequeathed in the 1920s by eccentric art collector Feliks Jasieński to Krakow's National Museum—fabrics, art, wood engravings and weapons. For little-known reasons, Jasieński dedicated his life seeking out artifacts from Japan. In storage for decades, the collection caught the interest of film director Andrzej Wajda and his wife, always keen to raise the cultural profile of the city. Upon their initiative, a riverside centre was built here to house both Jasieński's artifacts and host exhibitions by contemporary Japanese artists. Arata Isozaki's light-filled complex is the perfect backdrop for the 7,000-strong permanent collection, shown in rotation, and diverse temporary shows. Manggha also contains a hall, a terrace café and sushi bar. ⏲ *1 hr. Ul.Konopnickiej 26.* ☎ *012-267-27-03. www.manggha. krakow.pl. Admission 15zł/10zł. Tue–Sun 10am–6pm.*

⑤ **Manggha Sushi Café.** Some 15 varieties of sushi and a lovely riverside view are on offer at one of Krakow's best museum eateries. Ginger and other types of sake are also available, plus Japanese beers Asahi and Sapporo, and a range of teas too. *Ul.Konopnickiej 26* ☎ *012-267-2703. $$.*

⑥ ★ **Retmanski Stone Bridge.** Wander along the south bank of the Vistula from Manggha, past the Grunwald Bridge and you come to a bend in the river and this little stone bridge. A century old, it is named after the raftsman who would have used the waterway to trade goods. The scene is bucolic—the quiet Wilga tributary divides Podgórze from the rest of the south bank, where young couples skim stones and old men dangle fishing rods. Slated for redevelopment, the area should be best enjoyed before another leisure complex rises in its place. Another 10 minutes and you arrive at the **Piłsudski Bridge and Podgórze proper.** ⏲ *10 min. Zatorska/Przedwiesnie.*

⑦ **Piłsudski Bridge.** Opened in 1933, this cast-iron bridge rises in three arches across the river, allowing views of historic Wawel and newly regenerated Podgórze on either side. (See p 60). ⏲ *10 min.*

Krakow By Boat

Vistula tours: In summer, a handful of companies run trips along the river, usually setting off from Bulwar Czerwieński on the north bank of the Vistula at the foot of Wawel. The Nimfa makes regular hour tours around Krakow (12zł/10zł) or three-hour tour to Tyniec (20zł/15zł) at weekends. Check Żegluga Krakowska for details (☎ 012-422-08-55, www.zegluga.krakow.pl). Sobieski (☎ 012-452-23-04, www.ster.net.pl) also runs regular tourist boats to Tyniec and Bielany (2 hours). More haphazard but cheaper river trams (☎ 050-610-70-37, www.tramwajwodny.pl) head for Tyniec once there are enough passengers on board.

8 Mauretania. Moored by the northern foot of Piłsudski Bridge, this boat bar-restaurant is a handy stop-off from lunchtime to past bedtime. Pastas, salads, seafood and grilled meats can be accompanied by wines from France, Italy and the Ukraine, and followed by an extensive choice of cocktails. Below deck is all wood veneer and maritime-themed decoration—above is a view of Podgórze from the opposite bank. *Bulwar Kurlandzki. www.mauretania.biz. $.*

9 ★★ Pauline Church. The few who venture down to Kazimierz's far riverside edge are rewarded with this bizarre church and its impressive crypt. On this site in the 11th century, the more modest Church of St Michael witnessed the brutal murder of Stanisław Szczepański, bishop of Krakow. A curse fell upon the royal family responsible for the deed, giving rise to a multitude of superstitions and a much bigger Gothic church. This in turn was replaced by the imposing baroque church you see today. The crypt contains the tombs of artist Stanisław Wyspiański, composer Karol Szymanowski (1882–1937)and poet Adam Asnyk (1838–1897). 🕐 *1 hr. Ul.Skaleczna 15. ☎ 012-421-72-44. www.skalka. paulini.pl. Daily 9am–7pm.*

The century old Retmanski stone bridge.

Around the **Planty**

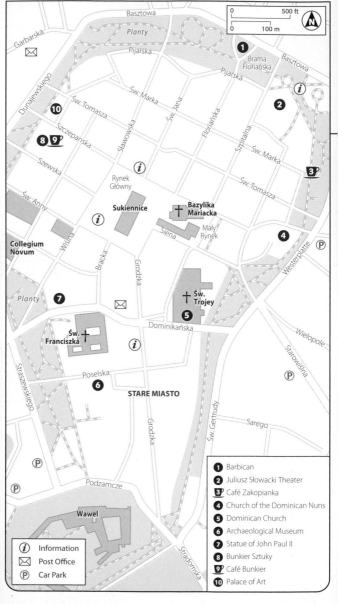

1 Barbican
2 Juliusz Słowacki Theater
3 Café Zakopianka
4 Church of the Dominican Nuns
5 Dominican Church
6 Archaeological Museum
7 Statue of John Paul II
8 Bunkier Sztuki
9 Café Bunkier
10 Palace of Art

(i) Information
⊠ Post Office
Ⓟ Car Park

It was the Austrians who decided to demolish Krakow's fortified ring in the early 1800s—and Cracovians who decided to create a unique, circular, public park in their place: Planty. Bookended by Wawel in the south, these public gardens encircle all the Old Town, a verdant ring of 4 km, some 20 hectares' worth, dotted with monuments, statues and plaques. Few locals pay them any attention. They are happy to plot up on one of the many park benches, with a book or a newspaper, and take advantage of urban green slap in the city centre. Cyclists, dog-walkers and lovers stroll along the concrete paths that criss-cross the gardens, heading either to or from the adjoining Old Town—or going nowhere at all in particular.

➊ ★ Barbican. Little accentuates Krakow's medieval appearance, and fear of invasion, more than this once mighty fortress and drawbridge built in the 1400s. The Barbican never saw action and today its grassed-over surrounds allow for a grand entrance into the Old Town from the north, or the ideal starting point for a leafy circumnavigation of Krakow's historic centre. (See p 18). 🕐 *20 min. Basztowa. All trams to Basztowa.*

➋ ★★★ Juliusz Słowacki Theater. Krakow's most prestigious concert hall is named after the 19th century romantic poet and dramatist who died in exile in Paris. A venue for classical music, dance and theater productions, this ornate fin-de-siècle building stands at the north-east corner of the Planty—in the north-west corner, the other side of the Barbican, is a monument to one of Słowacki's heroines, Lilla Weneda. 🕐 *20 min. Pl.Św.Ducha 1.* ☎ *012-424-45-00. www.slowacki.krakow.pl.*

Barbican provides a picturesque entrance into the Old Town.

The ornate fin-de-siècle Juliusz Słowacki Theatre.

3 **Café Zakopianka.** With its terrace offering a perfect view of the Planty, this historic, arty café has been in business since 1834. Snacks, draught Heineken from a huge beer tap and proper coffee from an elaborate machine from Hamburg-Altona offer sustenance and a continental atmosphere—French decorative touches do the rest. *Św.Marka 34.* ☎ *012-421-40-45. $.*

4 ★ **Church of the Dominican Nuns.** Dedicated to Our Lady of the Snow, this baroque nunnery church was consecrated in 1634, shortly after the convent's conversion from a government building. Its ownership, wrapped up in the politics of 17th-century Krakow, passed from the influential Tarnowski family, who sold it to the wealthy benefactor Anna Lubomirska, keen to find a home for the nuns. Our Lady of the Snow relates to Lubomirska's son, a Polish commander who defeated a stronger Turkish force in battle. Its prime attraction today is an icon of the Virgin dating from around the

same time. ⏱ *20 min. Ul.Mikołajska 21.* ☎ *012-422-79-25-51. Open for services.*

5 ★ **Dominican Church.** This unusual church was built in 1250, shortly after the Dominican order itself was founded. What you see today is a late 19th-century rebuild of the 13th-century Gothic original. Many of the ornate chapels survived an earlier fire, most notably the Myszkowski, with busts of the family lining the dome. It's very much an active church, with busy services. Some 100 Dominicans live and study here today. (See p 47) ⏱ *30 min. Stolarska 12* ☎ *012-423-16-13. Daily 8am–8pm.*

6 ★★★ **Archaeological Museum.** Set in grand grounds with Wawel in the background, this former Habsburg prison was opened as a Museum of the Antiquities in 1850. Its collection of Egyptian sarcophagi, figurines and cat mummies are discoveries made at El Hibeh from the 22nd dynasty. Resins from southern Poland are said to be used in the embalming process, although further explanation is not given. Dark corners reveal displays of coins, masks and pottery. Another of the three floors of this fusty but fascinating museum contains finds made around the Małopolska region, covering a dizzying array of historic periods. Despite the maps and models, the exhibits arenot fully documented and you walk past a blur of swords, bracelets and pots trying to link the life-like figures of early man with the tools and jewelry he created. It's all quite intriguing—you walk out to find a sunny spot to sit in the garden pleased that you'd paid the modest admission fee but somehow no wiser about Egypt or Małopolska. ⏱ *1 hr. Ul.Poselska 3.* ☎ *012-422-71-00. www.ma.krakow.pl. Admission 7zł/5zł*

7 Statue of John Paul II. Several statues have been erected to Poland's greatest modern-day hero around his adopted home town—this one stands in the courtyard of the Palace of Bishops where Karoly Wojtyla lived as a student, and stayed on his visits as Pope. It was was created in bronze soon after his election by Italian Jole Sensi Croci. Thousands of Cracovians filled the streets around here upon the news of Pope John Paul's death in April 2005. 🕐 *10 min. Ul.Franciszkanska 3.*

8 ★★★ Bunkier Sztuky. The Art Bunker is worth a look in whatever the time of year—the contemporary agenda of exhibitions at this attractive Modernist building changes regularly and can usually be relied on to be challenging and interesting. The café alone is worth a visit. 🕐 *30 min. Pl.Szczepański 3a.* ☎ *012-423-09-71. www.bunkier.com.pl.*

9 Café Bunkier. The finest place to sip coffee or sink a beer on the Planty is this terrace venue attached to the contemporary art

Café Bunkier.

gallery of the same name. For nine months of the year, transparent sheets protect customers from the elements, umbrella heaters taking the chill from the bitter Polish winter. In summer, the covers come off and the Bunkier floods with sunlight. Readings and screenings are staged here every now and then. *Pl.Szczepański 3a.* ☎ *012-431-05-85. $.*

10 Palace of Art. This building, the first example of Art Nouveau in Krakow, harks back to a time in the late 1800s when the city was awash with famous artists—Stanisław Wyspiański, Jan Matejko, and so on. When he designed it at the turn of the last century, Franciszek Mączyński (1874–1947) sought to express their struggle with his façade representing Doubt, Pain and Despair, with busts of these artists alongside. Exhibitions here tend to be more high-brow than the more cutting-edge shows at the Art Bunker nearby—but the building is well worth a look. 🕐 *15 min. Pl.Szczepański 4* ☎ *012-422-66-16.*

The Archaeological Museum's collection of Egyptian artifacts.

Salwator & **Zwierzyniec**

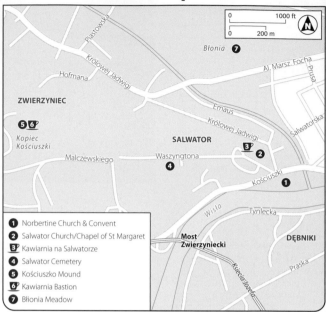

1 Norbertine Church & Convent
2 Salwator Church/Chapel of St Margaret
3' Kawiarnia na Salwatorze
4 Salwator Cemetery
5 Kościuszko Mound
6' Kawiarnia Bastion
7 Błonia Meadow

The terminus of three tram routes, Salwator is an easy
jump-off point for a hike into the open greenery of Zwierzyniec
west of Krakow. Attractions include the Kościuszko Mound and the
cemetery of Salwator, whose steep, crumbling streets were popular
with writers and artists before the war. A bohemian atmosphere still
hangs in the air—that is, until the developers move in.

**1 ★ Norbertine Church &
Convent.** Opposite the tram terminus by the river, stands this partly
Romanesque complex, a centre for
Norbertine sisters since 1148. Its
sturdy appearance harks back to
Jagellonian times when the church
needed protection from invaders.
White-dressed canonesses still live
here but the church opens for afternoon services. This is the starting
point for June's Lajkonik parade. Dating from the Tartar invasions, the
carnival is led by a bearded man in
a pointy hat who leads a crowd in
medieval costume by hobby horse,

Python-style. The procession ends
at the market square ⏱ *15 min. Ul.T
Kościuszki. Trams 1, 2, 6: Salwator.*

**2 ★ Salwator Church/Chapel
of St Margarest.** Climbing steep,
winding Św.Bronistwy, you find two
facing churches: Salwator and the
Chapel of St Margaret. The former
contains Romanesque elements
and, on the wall of the Presbytery,
frescoes from the 16th century. St
Margaret's Chapel, a wooden struc-
ture on a hilly slope, dates from the
late 1600s. In March 2008, a statue
of John Paul II was erected outside.

🕐 *20 min. Św.Bronisłwy. Trams 1, 2, 6: Salwator.*

3 **Kawiarnia na Salwatorze.** On the steep slope to Salwator Cemetery, this pretty, garden café offers draught Bitburger, cakes, snacks, and local history. This is the house of Władysław Anczyc (1823–1883), the 19th-century Polish poet—the adjoining street is named after him. Imprisoned by the Austrians in 1846, Anczyc was a prominent member of Salwator's artistic community. *Św. Bronisławy/Anczycza 1.* ☎ *0602-67-13-15. $.*

Norbertine Church and Convent.

4 ★ **Salwator Cemetery.** As Św.Bronisławy becomes flat, straight, tree-lined Aleja Waszyntona, this quiet cemetery appears on the left-hand side—and with it, a wonderful view of Krakow and beyond. Visit on the Day of the Dead, November 1, and the gravestones will be haloed in candlelight. Consecrated in 1865, Salwator contains the tombs of painters and writers who lived here before the Second World War. 🕐 *30 min. Al.J.Waszyngtona.*

5 ★★★ **kids** **Kościuszko Mound.** Accessed by the half-hourly minibus 100 from the Salwator terminus, this panoramic attraction contains several features. Foremost is the **Kościuszko Mound** itself, a conical hill erected in the 1820s, in honor of the soldier who fought for Polish and American independence. A spiral staircase leads to the top—it's a dizzying climb. At the foot stands the neo-Gothic Chapel of Św.Bronisława, built by the Austrians in the 1850s. Round the corner is a waxworks museum (8zł/6zł), a disappointing collection of Polish heroes in familiar poses. A further museum beside the Bastion café within the mound complex displays the life and achievements of Tadeusz Kościuszko, the development of the mound and a history of this local phenomenon. On one wall is a panoramic shot taken of the nearby Błonia Meadow packed for Pope John Paul II's visit. 🕐 *1 hr. Al.Waszyngtona 1.* ☎ *012-425-11-16. www.kopieckosciuszko.pl. Admission 6–8zł/4zł. Free national holidays of Mar 24, May 3 and Nov 11. Daily 9am–dusk. Museum daily 9.30am–4.30pm. Bus 100: Kopiec Kościuszko.*

6 **Kawiarnia Bastion.** At the lower slope of the mound is this twin-terrace open-air café, serving drinks and snacks. Overlooking the fortifications, it displays a replica of the Racławice Panorama, the battle scene of the Kościuszko Uprising housed in Wrocław. *Al.Waszyngtona 1.* ☎ *012-425-11-16. $.*

7 ★★ **kids** **Błonia Meadow.** Signposted from the Kościuszko Mound, this large, green space is a winding 10-min. walk down V.Hofmana to the main Królowej Jadwigi road. Criss-crossed by hiking and cycle paths, the meadow is used by kite-flyers and Frisbee throwers—don't expect cafés or ice-cream stands. Some 2 million Poles gathered in 2002 for the last mass Pope John Paul II gave here. 🕐 *30 min. Buses 134, 152, 192, 292.*

Las Wolski

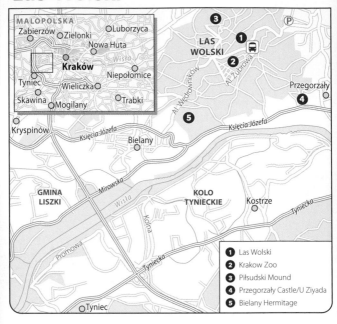

1. Las Wolski
2. Krakow Zoo
3. Piłsudski Mound
4. Przegorzały Castle/U Ziyada
5. Bielany Hermitage

At Krakow's far western edge, the open woodland of Las Wolski contains well-marked hiking trails and a handful of attractions including the city zoo. At its southern fringe, on the eastern tip is Przegorzały Castle; on the western side is the bizarre Camadulensian Hermitage of Bielany. Regular buses from the city centre serve the area—hiking between them would take the best part of a day, no bad way to spend time away from the downtown bustle.

1 ★ **kids** **Las Wolski.** Best accessed by the 134 bus, which runs right from the Cracovia Hotel and terminates at its main attraction, the zoo, this 1,000-acre area of natural woodland was opened for public recreation 100 years ago. By the entrance to the zoo is a map showing hiking routes, the main sites and the times it takes to walk to them. From this vantage point you can easily reach the Piłsudski Mound, Przegorzały Castle and Bielany. 🕐 *2 hr. Bus 134: Zoo.*

2 ★★★ **kids** **Krakow Zoo.** Respected internationally as a top breeding zoo, Krakow's animal park has been in business for 80 years. Snow leopards, Andean condors, wild cats and lynxes have all been raised here in captivity. Local species include boar and bison. A snack bar by the main entrance overlooks the elephant enclosure.

Krakow Zoo wild cat.

(See p 43). ⏱ *2 hr. Las Wolski* ☎ *012-425-35-51. Admission 14zł/7zł. Daily Summer 9am–7pm. Spring, Autumn Daily 9am–6pm. Winter Daily 9am–3pm. Bus 134: Zoo.*

❸ ★ kids Piłsudski Mound. A signposted 15-minute walk from the zoo stands the tallest and most recent of Krakow's many mounds. Named after the national hero who led the country to independence in the First World War, and who died shortly before the mound was finished and opened in 1937, Piłsudski contains soil from the major battlefields where Poles fought between 1914 and 1918. Its size has protected it—both the Nazis and the Soviets wished to raze it. The latter succeeded in removing it from most maps and destroying the tablet laid by the Polish Legion. Prompted by the Solidarity movement, the mound was gradually restored, soil added from the battlefields of the Second World War. It was reopened with an elaborate ceremony in 2002. ⏱ *1 hr. Free admission.*

❹ Przegorzally Castle/U Ziyada. At the far south-eastern edge of Las Wolski, located over the river, stands the mock historic Przegorzally Castle. Used for recreation by the Nazis, the castle now contains the restaurant U Ziyada, which serves Polish standards and Kurdish specialties—a hint at the nationality of the current owner. *Ul.Jodłowa 13.* ☎ *012-429-71-05. $$.*

The terrace of Przegorzaly Castle in Krakow, Poland with the valley and Vustula river below.

Hermitage of the Camaldolese Monks.

5 ★ **Bielany Hermitage.** At the creepy but authentic Bielany Hermitage women are only allowed on certain feast days—most notably Christmas, Whit Sunday, Easter Sunday and Monday. Such arcane rules echo Camadulensian order who still occupy the hermitage complex. Men are admitted at 10 specific times between 8am and 4pm, and then only to the hermitage church and crypt. Here the bones of the hermits' predecessors are stacked away in niches, to be buried decades after their passing. The monks lead quiet lives of privation in basic cabins behind the church. ⏲ *30 min. Free admission. Bus 109: Bielany.* ●

Practical Matters

If you're in the Las Wolski area, a hour's hike over the Vistula will bring you to Tyniec Abbey—there are also day trips straight from Krakow. Tourists come to wander around the 11th-century Benedictine Abbey, spectacularly located over the limestone cliffs at the water's edge. There are also organ recitals here in July and August. Contact the abbey at Benedyktynska 37 (☎ 012-688-52-00).

Dining Best Bets

Best **Breakfast**
★ Metropolitan $$ *Ul.Sławkowska 3*
(p 106)

Best **Wine List**
★★ Vinoteka La Bodega $$
Ul.Sławkowska 12 (p 110)

Best **Italian**
★★ Aqua e Vino $$$ *Ul.Wiślna 5-10*
(p 110)

Best **Seafood**
★★ Farina $$ *Ul.Św.Marka 16*
(p 104)

Best **Comfort Food**
★ Bar Grodzki $ *Ul.Grodzka 47*
(p 102)

Best **Authentic Jewish
Atmosphere**
★ Klezmer Hois $$ *Ul.Szeroka 6*
(p 105)

Best **Pierogi**
★ Pierożki u Vincenta $ *Ul.Józefa
11 (p 107)*

Best **Reliably Expensive**
★★ Wentzl $$$ *Rynek Glówny 19*
(p 110)

Best **Terrace View**
★ Klub Panorama $
Ul.Zwierzyniecka 50 (p 106)

Best **Pizzeria**
★ Trzy Papryczki $ *Ul.Poselska 17*
(p 109)

Best **Polish Regional**
★ Jarema $$ *Pl.Matejki 5 (p 105)*

Best **Waitstaff**
★★★ Miód Malina $$ *Ul.Grodzka
40 (p 106)*

Best **Gourmet French**
★★★ Cyrano de Bergerac $$$$
Ul.Sławkowska 26, (p 104)

Best **Hotel Restaurant**
★★★ Copernicus $$$$ *Hotel
Copernicus, Ul.Kanonicza 16 (p 103)*

Best **Piano Acccompaniment**
★ Jarema $ *Pl.Matejki 5 (p 105)*

Best **Latin American**
★ Manzana $$ *Ul.Miodowa 11*
(p 106)

Best **Soups**
★ Senacka $$ *Ul.Grodzka 5 (p 109)*

Best **Vodka Selection**
★ Starka $$ *Ul.Józefa 14 (p 109)*

Best **Salads**
★ Vega $ *Ul.Krupnicza 22 (p 110)*

Best **for Extravagant Meat
Sauces**
Pod Aniołami $$$ *Ul,Grodzka 35*
(p 107)

Best Hotel Restaurant: Copernicus.

Central Dining

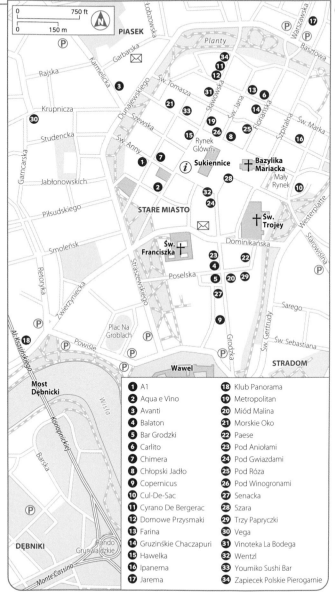

1 A1	**18** Klub Panorama
2 Aqua e Vino	**19** Metropolitan
3 Avanti	**20** Miód Malina
4 Balaton	**21** Morskie Oko
5 Bar Grodzki	**22** Paese
6 Carlito	**23** Pod Aniołami
7 Chimera	**24** Pod Gwiazdami
8 Chłopski Jadło	**25** Pod Róza
9 Copernicus	**26** Pod Winogronami
10 Cul-De-Sac	**27** Senacka
11 Cyrano De Bergerac	**28** Szara
12 Domowe Przysmaki	**29** Trzy Papryczki
13 Farina	**30** Vega
14 Gruzińskie Chaczapuri	**31** Vinoteka La Bodega
15 Hawelka	**32** Wentzl
16 Ipanema	**33** Yourmiko Sushi Bar
17 Jarema	**34** Zapiecek Polskie Pierogarnie

Kazimierz & Podgórze Dining

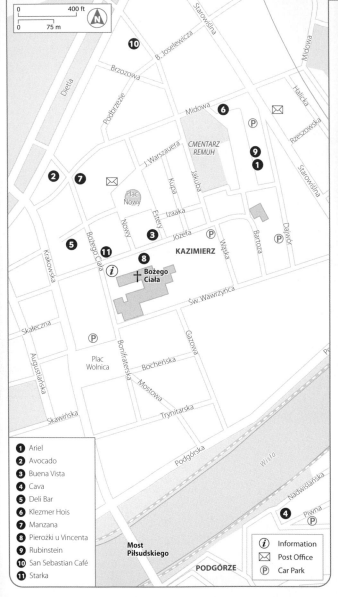

0 — 400 ft	
0 — 75 m	

Starowiślna
B. Joselewicza
Midowa
Halicka
Brzozowa
Dietla
Podbrzezie
Rzeszowska
Midowa
CMENTARZ REMUH
Starowiślna
J.Warszauera
Kupa
Jakuba
Plac Nowy
Nowy
Estery
Izaaka
Dajwór
Bożego Ciała
Józefa
Wąska
Bartoza
KAZIMIERZ
Krakowska
Bożego Ciała
Bożego Ciała
Św. Wawrzyńca
Skałeczna
Plac Wolnica
Bonifraterska
Bocheńska
Gazowa
Augustiańska
Mostowa
Skawińska
Trynitarska
Podgórska
Wisła
Nadwiślańska
Piwna
Most Piłsudskiego
PODGÓRZE

1 Ariel
2 Avocado
3 Buena Vista
4 Cava
5 Deli Bar
6 Klezmer Hois
7 Manzana
8 Pierożki u Vincenta
9 Rubinstein
10 San Sebastian Café
11 Starka

ⓘ Information
✉ Post Office
Ⓟ Car Park

Krakow Dining **A to Z**

A1 OLD TOWN *SUSHI/INTERNATIONAL*   Opened in 2008, this sister restaurant to La Cantina in Katowice serves sushi, cocktails and global delights (Provençal frogs' legs, snails, paella, New Zealand lamb) to moneyed guests on a quiet University Quarter terrace or long glitzy interior. Currently boasts the most extensive sushi selection in town. *Ul.Jagellońska/ul.Św.Anny* ☎ *012-429-50-12. Entrees 19–89zł. AE, DC, MC, V. Lunch & dinner daily. Map p 99.*

★★ Aqua e Vino OLD TOWN *ITALIAN*   Suitable candidate for best Italian in town, creative, contemporary 'Water and Wine' has set consistently high standards since opening in 2005. Specializing in dishes from the Veneto region, Francesco and Roberto's chic eaterie also offers quality Italian wines. It's a lounge bar too, so order up one of four dozen cocktails before tucking into fresh ravioli with venison and black-truffle pesto or pork fillet in gorgonzola sauce. *Ul.Wiślna 5-10.* ☎ *012-421-25-67. Entrees 22–74zł. AE, DC, MC, V. Lunch & dinner daily. Map p 99.*

★ Ariel KAZIMIERZ *JEWISH* Tourist flock to this homely favorite in the heart of the Kazimierz, partly because of the well-produced Jewish standards (matzaball soup, roast goose, gefilte fish), partly because of the atmosphere akin to a grandmother's drawing room. There are Israeli wines too, kosher vodkas and Passover slivovicz spirit. *Ul. Szeroka 17-18.* ☎ *012-421-79-20. Entrees 18–47zł. AE, DC, MC, V. Lunch & dinner daily. Map p 100.*

★★ Avanti BY OLD TOWN *ITALIAN* Set in the rapidly trendifying neighborhood just outside the Old Town

Jewish favourites at Ariel.

in the student quarter, Avanti comprises a top-quality restaurant, a garden café and orangerie with its own extensive menu. The food is sublime, whether the grilled prawns on mixed salad, the seafood spaghetti with pesto or the veal in porcini mushroom sauce. Fabulous selection of coffees with liqueur sauces too. *Ul.Karmelicka 7.* ☎ *012-430-07-70. Entrees 19–20zł. AE, DC, MC, V. Lunch from 1pm & dinner daily. Map p 99.*

Avocado KAZIMIERZ *INTERNATIONAL*   Sunlight floods through this bright, contemporary space— the perfect spot to enjoy light, continental dishes and rub shoulders with a discerning young crowd. French influences stand out on the menu (the secret recipe fish soup from Marseille, the Café de Paris sirloin steak) and a wine list headed by a decent Chablis. Naturally, avocados

Classic, old-school service at Balaton.

feature too, in a salad with marinated salmon and in the cream soup. Grab a spot on the front terrace in warmer weather. *Ul.Bożego Ciała 1.* ☎ *012-422-04-86. Entrees 16–55zł. AE, DC, MC, V. Lunch & dinner daily. Map p 100.*

Balaton OLD TOWN *HUNGARIAN*
It's been here for decades, this classic Magyar haunt with its wooden, two-room interior and old-school waiters. The food remains authentic, the roast duck, the wild-boar stew and the bean soup. Prices are as cheap as you'll find for such quality fare so centrally located, and that includes the wines (Bull's Blood, Kékfrankos, Tokaj dessert variety). If you opt for one of the dishes for two (60zł), make sure you bring a substantial appetite. *Ul.Grodzka 37.* ☎ *012-422-04-69. Entrees 10–30zł. AE, DC, MC, V. Lunch & dinner daily. Map p 99.*

★ **Bar Grodzki** OLD TOWN. *POLISH*
The menu board in English and Polish at this perennial local cheapie tells all. A list of domestic standards, most for under 10zl, attracts a regular crowd of budget-conscious diners, workers and backpackers. Bigos

cabbage-and-sausage stew, pancakes and pierogi all feature, served in a tiled interior decked out with little rustic touches. If you're feeling flush, splash out on the 14.90zł pork chop and potatoes. *Ul.Grodzka 47.* ☎ *012-422-68-07. Entrees 8–14.90zł. No credit cards. Lunch & dinner till 7pm daily. Map p 99.*

★ **Buena Vista** KAZIMIERZ *CUBAN*
Slap on Plac Nowy this Cuban-themed eaterie makes a nice change from all that noise and grunge—and a kitchen till 11.30pm is handy too. The shredded beef and tomato favorite *ropa vieja* is the stand-out of the modest list of mains, with lemon, coconut and prawn the tastiest of the soups. Chicken is the only children's choice. Disappointingly, beers are Polish, Dutch or Irish, with a limited choice of rums, but a 10-strong choice of mojitos (apple, melon, strawberry) make up for it. *Ul.Józefa 26.* ☎ *0668-03-50-00. Entrees 21–35zł. AE, DC, MC, V. Lunch & dinner daily. Map p 100.*

★ **Carlito** OLD TOWN *ITALIAN*
The terrace perched above Floriański is the ideal spot to tuck into one of 10 pizzas, 10 pastas and half-a-dozen seafood dishes. Big spenders

Carlito's terrace for an ideal summer spot.

can order duck breast with marsala figs (42zł) but most are happy to share a four-piece Carlito pizza with friends and enjoy the view. The pretty, expansive interior fills in winter. *Ul.Floriańska 28.* ☎ *012-429-19-12. Entrees 14–42zł. AE, DC, MC, V. Lunch & dinner daily. Map p 99.*

★ **kids Cava** PODGÓRZE *MEDITER-RANEAN* Podgórze's up-and-coming status suits this chic café-restaurant, opened in September 2007. Fashion TV plays as young professionals tuck into truffle pasta and the specialty dish of snails, prepared French-, Italian- or Thai-style. A display of peppers, salamis and cheeses indicates the quality of the breakfasts (served until 11.30am) and salads, while kids can happily snack away at toast or a baguette. Cava also operates as a bar, serving the titular Spanish prosecco, mojitos and Mediterranean wines. *Ul.Nadwiślańska 1.* ☎ *012-656-74-56. Entrees 16–66zł. AE, DC, MC, V. Breakfast, lunch & dinner daily. Map p 100.*

kids Chimera OLD TOWN *POLISH* Professors from the nearby university buildings frequent this long-established Polish favorite. Chimera offers the widest selection of salads in town from a display lining one of four dining rooms, but most come for the hearty duck and goose. Children's theatre performances are occasionally given on Sunday mornings. *Ul.Św.Anny 3.* ☎ *012-423-21-78. Entrees 22–78zł. AE, DC, MC, V. Lunch & dinner daily. Map p 99.*

Chłopskie Jadło OLD TOWN *POLISH* With branches all over Poland, and four around Krakow, Chłopskie Jadło is a reliable purveyor of traditional local cuisine. A vast range of favorites is offered in suitably rustic surroundings—there are 20 soups alone. Specialties include pork roast or pork ribs, both with Silesian

Chłopskie Jadło for traditional, local cuisine.

dumplings, bigos stew with mushrooms and various meats, and cabbage leaves stuffed with rice and meat in a tomato sauce. Trout is another dish prepared according to a house recipe. If this branch is busy, try the one nearby at Grodzka 9. *Ul.Św.Jana 3.* ☎ *012-429-51-57. AE, DC, MC, V. Lunch & dinner daily. Map p 99.*

★★★ **Copernicus** OLD TOWN *POLISH/COSMOPOLITAN* If Vaclav Havel or Roman Polański is in town, this is where they dine. Amid frescoes and beneath a Renaissance ceiling, an attentive staff serve superbly conceived seasonal dishes such as veal with marinated tongue on a truffle and potato mousse,or duck with foie gras spiced with marjoram. It's a favorite for weddings, when the wine bar patio comes into its own. Guests at other Likus hotels—the Pod Róza, the Stary and this one—receive a 10 percent discount. *Ul.Kanonicza 16, Copernicus Hotel.* ☎ *012-424-34-21. Entrees 69–129zł. AE, DC, MC, V. Lunch & dinner daily. Map p 99.*

The superior hotel restaurant at Cul De Sac.

★★ Cul-De-Sac OLD TOWN *POLISH/INTERNATIONAL* Another of Krakow's superior hotel restaurants, this lower-floor venue displays medieval finds discovered as the Gródek was being converted into the stylish lodging it is today. Choose between a table in the leafy conservatory or main room flooded with natural light as you consider duck with grilled apples in rose sauce, or poultry vol-au-vent with steamed oyster mushrooms in cream. The starter of home-made tagliatelle with rabbit ragout in rosemary sauce is a full meal in itself—especially if you open your meal with crayfish soup and steamed leeks. Seasonal vegetables are used throughout and the service is suitably stellar. *Ul.Na Gródzku 4, Hotel Gródek.* ☎ *012-431-90–30. Entrees 45–79zł. AE, DC, MC, V. Lunch & dinner daily. Map p 99.*

★★ Cyrano de Bergerac OLD TOWN *FRENCH* One of the best restaurants in Poland, and certainly the top French table in town, the exclusive Cyrano serves banquet-worthy dishes in a historic medieval cellar. Foie gras with caramelized pear and blackcurrant sauce, Châteaubriand with three-pepper sauce, cognac flambé and warm fresh vegetables, and St Jaques scallops with fettuccine and pesto sauce, are typical dishes. An impressive, French-only wine selection rounds off the experience. *Ul.Sławkowska 26.* ☎ *012-411-72-88. Entrees 43–95zł. AE, DC, MC, V. Lunch & dinner Mon–Sat. Closed Sun. Map p 99.*

Deli Bar KAZIMIERZ *HUNGARIAN* Opened in January 2008, this cheap, authentic Magyar eaterie comprises a dining room and separate bar with fruit machines. As for the food, all the Hungarian favorites are here—catfish stew, schnitzel, breaded mushrooms—along with a breakfast (9am–noon) selection of scrambled eggs, frankfurters and the hangover-curing sausage-and-tomato stew. Wines come from Eger, Tokaj and Szekszárd, the draught beer from Poland. *Ul.Meiselsa 5* ☎ *012-430-64-04 Entrees 8–25zł. No credit cards. Breakfast, lunch & dinner daily. Map p 100.*

Domowe Przysmaki OLD TOWN *POLISH* Nothing costs more than 10zł on this menu—no wonder this simple, rustic restaurant is a favorite with backpackers and budget-conscious locals. For 8zł a steaming plate of pierogi (with cabbage and mushrooms, cottage cheese and potatoes or meat), stuffed cabbage or fried chese will be plonked in front of you. There are toasted sandwiches for those with smaller appetites. *Ul.Sławkowska 24a.* ☎ *012-422-57-51. Entrees 8–10zł. No credit cards. Lunch & dinner until 9pm daily. Map p 99.*

★ kids Farina OLD TOWN *SEAFOOD* Krakow's premier fish restaurant makes imaginative use of imported delicacies from Brittany and Italy. And, given the quality and contemporary setting, prices are reasonable too—grilled trout with garlic and almonds, shrimp fettucine and spaghetti frutti di mare are below 30zł. Farina specializes in whole fish baked with garlic and herbs, such as John Dory, Dover sole and sea bream. Order lobster five days in advance. The kids' menu (5–14zł) offers a good choice too. *Ul.Św.Marka 16.* ☎ *012-422-16-80. Entrees 19–170zł. AE, DC, MC, V. Lunch & dinner daily. Map p 99.*

Gruzińskie Chaczapuri OLD TOWN *GEORGIAN* Some two dozen Georgian dishes are available at each of Krakow's five branches of the Chaczapuri chain. Cheese, pork, chicken and aubergine all feature strongly on a menu where little costs more than 20zł, presented with tasty Georgian seasoning. Vegetarians are well catered for, with a handful of tasty tomato-and-pepper based stews. Look out also for the Georgian salad with cheese and cabbage. Kindzmarauli and Makuzani wines are available by the glass. *Ul.Floriańska 26.* ☎ *012-292-02-44. Entrees 14–23.50zł. AE, DC, MC, V. Lunch & dinner daily. Map p 99.*

Hawelka OLD TOWN *POLISH* This is the most famous place in town— you're not just here for the pricy beef tenderloins but the Habsburg ambiance and 130-year-old tradition. It's a coffeehouse too, so you can admire the sepia murals and portrait of Franz Josef without having to splash out on a 70zł steak. Salmon, wild boar and chicken are heavily featured on an extensive menu, but leave room for desserts such as ice-cream soufflé with dried fruit and nuts in cranberry sauce. Terrace space from spring onwards. *Rynek Główny 34.* ☎ *012-422-06-31. Entrees 19–89zł. AE, DC, MC, V. Breakfast, lunch & dinner daily. Map p 99.*

Ipanema OLD TOWN *BRAZILIAN* Krakow's solitary Brazilian eaterie is suitably bright and breezy, its menu ranging from traditional bean stew to shark steak and lobster. There are African touches too, with cassava and thick coconut sauce accompanying pork and chicken. Much is served with rice and polenta, so you won't leave hungry, but peppers and spicy sauces relieve any blandness. Spirits include cachaça, cocktails and mixed drinks several varieties of caipirinha. *Ul.Św.Tomasza 28.* ☎ *012-422-53-23. Entrees 19–89zł. AE, DC, MC, V. Lunch from 1pm & dinner daily. Map p 99.*

★ **Jarema** NEAR OLD TOWN *POLISH/LITHUANIAN* Specializing in dishes from eastern Poland and Lithuania, this is a lovely, traditional venue on a quiet square five minutes from the Old Town. A piano tinkles as your smiling waitress presents you with a free appetizer of rustic bread and lard and a well-conceived menu featuring Lithuanian chilled crayfish soup, Lithuanian pork chops and black pudding with onion and apples. Game is well represented, rabbit or hare prepared in tasty creamy sauces. Drinks include a delicious dark *kwas*, non-alcoholic bready beer. *Pl.Matejki 5.* ☎ *012-429-36-69. Entrees 18–64zł. AE, DC, MC, V. Lunch & dinner daily. Map p 99.*

★ **Klezmer Hois** KAZIMIERZ *JEWISH* This landmark venue is a café, restaurant, theatre, hotel and music venue in one, its three public rooms dressed like a 19th-century drawing room of framed paintings and heavy tapestries. As concerns the restaurant, Jewish favorites such as berdytchov and matzaball soups, stuffed goose necks and cholent all feature, complemented by salads from turnip to horseradish. All comes with authentic musical accompaniment in the evenings—this is no sad old tourist trap. *Ul. Szeroka 6.*

☎ 012-411-12-45. Entrees 18.50–39zł. AE, DC, MC, V. Lunch & dinner daily. Map p 100.

★ **Klub Panorama** NOWY ŚWIAT POLISH   Hands down best terrace view in Krakow, the aptly named Panorama sits atop the riverside Jubilat shopping centre. The management could double the prices and still be justified—most meat and fish dishes here are in the 20zł range, There is a daily special at 15zł, salads, pricier grilled meats and several soups, including the cream forest mushroom variety served in a bowl of home-made bread. Celeriac with nuts and red cabbage with raisins are among the side dishes. Take in sunset with one of 30 cocktails. *Ul.Zwierzyniecka 50, Jubilat shopping center.* ☎ 012-422-28-14. Entrees 15–32zł. AE, DC, MC, V. Lunch & dinner daily. Map p 99.

★ **Manzana** KAZIMIERZ MEXICAN/ INTERNATIONAL   One half cocktail bar, one half restaurant, 'Apple' is a chic new Latin American spot in Kazimierz. A basic five dishes of fish and meat are complemented by a handful of soups, salads and appetizers. The thick black-bean with baby shrimp soup is hearty enough see you struggle with a main of fresh tuna steak afterwards—a more delicate Cancún shrimp cocktail may be a better starter. Watch out for the weekend specials, such as mussels in spicy sauce, and side dishes such as marinated fresh spinach. Latin and Polish cocktails can be enjoyed in both bar and restaurant, as can the evening-only bar menu. *Ul. Miodowa 11.* ☎ 012-422-22-77. Entrees 24–64zł. AE, DC, MC, V. Breakfast, lunch & dinner daily. Map p 100.

★ kids **Metropolitan** OLD TOWN COSMOPOLITAN   South African chef Des Davies runs this downtown, cosmopolitan bar-diner, where

Cosmopolitan cuisine at Metropolitan.

breakfast is as popular as lunch and dinner. Bagels, fry-ups and classic American burgers boast a quality of presentation carried over to the modest but well chosen lunch menu (Metropolitan beef fillet in cognac sauce, whole roasted trout with apple-and-parsnip stuffing) and wider dinner selection (seared duck breast confit with grilled polenta, pan-seared salmon fillet). Asian touches figure throughout, such as in the spicy Thai noodles and spicy Thai coconut soup. Look out for the house fish soup, a delicious mix of mussels, shrimps, saffron and Pernod. Wines come by the bottle or 150ml measure. *Ul.Sławkowska 3.* ☎ 012-421-98-03. Entrees 23–87zł. AE, DC, MC, V. Breakfast, lunch & dinner daily. Map p 99.

★★★ **Miód Malina** OLD TOWN POLISH   The queues outside the front door year round are no coincidence—reserve a table or miss out on one of Krakow's finest meals. And it's not just the wood-stove prepared roasted pork knuckle with fried cabbage or spare ribs marinated with honey and special plum sauce—the staff are sweethearts. To push the boat out, plump for the golden brown duck breast in mushroom-and-plum sauce followed by traditional Polish cheesecake, served warm *Ul.Grodzka 40.* ☎ *012-430-04-11. Entrees 18–64zł. AE, DC, MC, V. Lunch & dinner daily. Map p 99.*

Morskie Oko OLD TOWN *ZAKOPANE* Cartwheels, horse harnesses and peasant paraphernalia add suitable decoration to this cabin-like basement, where the regional cuisine of Zakopane is the prime attraction. Pork cutlet Zakopane-style, goulash soup with mushrooms and paprika, and sauerkraut soup with beetroot make a welcome change from domestic fare elsewhere around the Old Town. There are shashlik grills too. Meals are taken on heavy wooden tables, served by a waitstaff in traditional costume. In the bar upstairs you can also tuck into bloody sausage or bigos hunter's stew over a mug of beer. *Pl.Szczepański 8.* ☎ *012-431-24-23. Entrees 12–41zł. AE, DC, MC, V. Lunch & dinner daily. Map p 99.*

★ **Paese** OLD TOWN *CORSICAN* Poland's only Corsican restaurant has been in business for two decades, serving Calvi-style fiet mignon with Roquefort sauce and African catfish in leek sauce to four rooms of satisfied diners. Soups include Provençal with onions and a cheese variety with croutons, and the outstanding main dish (for three) is a beef fondue with three dips. There are four vegetarian dishes too. Corsican Cellier des Iles wine comes by the well-priced carafe or glass. Leave room for fiadone, Corsican cheesecake with rum. *Ul.Posel-ski 24.* ☎ *012-421-62-73. Entrees 19–40zł. AE, DC, MC, V. Lunch & dinner daily. Map p 99.*

★ **Pierożki u Vincenta** KAZ-IMIERZ *POLISH* Pierogi is the name of the game here, the Polish national dish of dumplings filled with any number of ingredients—in this case, 31 varieties, many not available anywhere else: lentil and pineapple; chicken liver and apple; and fried plums and cinnamon. There are a range of sauces too, fried bacon, sour cream, butter, plus a meat, vegetable and fruit platters for communal dining. Van Gogh's blue swirls decorate the side room that deals with the overflow from the cramped main area. *Ul.Józefa 11.* ☎ *012-430-68-34. Entrees 7–12zł. AE, DC, MC, V. Lunch & dinner daily. Map p 100.*

★ **Pod Aniołami** OLD TOWN *POLISH* Superior versions of traditional Polish classics is the attraction here—that, and a beautiful setting in an 18th-century Old-Town building with a courtyard garden. Game is well represented—wild boar with beech-smoked bacon, red cabbage and grilled pepper, and saddle of doe with cognac, stewed mushrooms, red cabbage and raisins in wine. This is local fare at its most rich and opulent, prepared in a beech-wood oven. Desserts include warm apple pie with egg liqueur and cheesecake with raspberry mousse. *Ul.Grodzka 35.* ☎ *012-421-39-99. Entrees 23–73zł. AE, DC, MC, V. Lunch & dinner daily. Map p 99.*

Miód Malina for great food and service.

Pod Gwiazdami OLD TOWN *POLISH* This off-main-square restaurant is often free when many venues nearby are packed. Regular visitors include guests of RT Hotels (the Rezydent here or Regent in Kazimierz), who receive a 20 percent discount. Prices are reasonable anyway, given the location, neither veal roast in herb sauce nor trout in almonds breaking the 30zł barrier. Chef's recommendations include pork loin with plums and trout rolls on spinach, while soups include żur of fermented rye and egg and sausage, and the Staropolska potato variety. Sepia prints of Krakow offer a nice decorative touch. *Ul.Grodzka 5, Hotel Rezydent.* ☎ *012-430-26-57. Entrees 12–30zł. AE, DC, MC, V. Lunch & dinner daily. Map p 99.*

Pod Róza OLD TOWN *POLISH/ INTERNATIONAL* The signature restaurant of a landmark hotel exudes suitable grandeur, located in a leafy, light-filled atrium dominating the lobby. The menu is seasonal, mainly Polish, with plenty of game and mushrooms in the autumn and salads in summer. The pierogi are home-made and a notch above elsewhere in the Old Town. Don't miss out on dessert—warm chocolate cake with pineapple mousse, lemon cake with mascarpone cream or a selection of home-made sorbets. *Ul.Floriańska 14, Hotel Pod Róza.* ☎ *012-424-33-00. Entrees 39–89zł. AE, DC, MC, V. Lunch & dinner daily. Map p 99.*

★★ **Pod Winogronami** OLD TOWN *POLISH/INTERNATIONAL* Chef Lorenzo Pilia oversees one of Krakow's finest Italian kitchens, a key element of the five-star Palac Bonerowski Hotel off the main square. The lamb chops in Sardinian myrtle, the spaghetti with half-a-lobster, the grilled tuna on salad with pecorino cheese and pesto, all reassuringly expensive and exquisitely

presented, There is a French element too, sole with caviar, prawns and Dijon mustard, and frogs' legs with pepperoni sauce. *Ul.Św.Jana 1, Hotel Palac Bonerowski.* ☎ *012-374-13-10. Entrees 35–139zł. AE, DC, MC, V. Lunch & dinner daily. Map p 99.*

★ **Rubinstein** KAZIMIERZ *INTERNATIONAL* The most upscale of the cluster of hotels in Kazimierz offers a refreshingly unpretentious, international selection of dishes at its terrace restaurant. Chef Adam Liburski has composed a balanced menu—beef soup with Lithuanian dumplings, vitello tonato, Galician poultry livers—with affordable alternatives in each category and three vegetarian options. *Ul.Szeroka 12.* ☎ *012-384-00-00. Entrees 25–82zł. AE, DC, MC, V. Lunch & dinner daily. Map p 100.*

San Sebastian Café KAZIMIERZ *INTERNATIONAL* Nothing more adventurous than a decent fill-up from breakfast through to bedtime, in a friendly, pub-like atmosphere. An English fry-up or omelets savory or sweet start the day, with ciabattas or salads for brunch. A dozen meat dishes (beef fillet with rosemary, pork

Rubinstein's terrace restaurant.

fillet glazed in honey) in the 50zł range make for a hearty evening meal, washed down with wines from Sicily or Israel. *Ul.Św.Sebastiana 25.* ☎ *012-429-24-76. Entrees 20–71zł. AE, DC, MC, V. Breakfast, lunch & dinner daily. Map p 100.*

★ **Senacka** OLD TOWN *POLISH* It may be grand, set in a decent Old-Town hotel, but this rather formal restaurant is relatively affordable, given the quality of Polish fare on offer. Roast duck with hot red cabbage, chicken in orange with rice and green beans, pork loin with forest mushrooms, are as well executed as you'll find most anywhere. Mention must be made of the soups—rabbit with egg yolk and horseradish, spicy goulash, homemade chicken with noodles—which are worth the visit alone. *Ul.Grodzka 5, Hotel Senacki.* ☎ *012-422-76-86. Entrees 14–59zł. AE, DC, MC, V. Lunch & dinner daily. Map p 99.*

Starka KAZIMIERZ *POLISH* This splendid bar-restaurant opened in 2007 offers quality Polish standards in informal, contemporary surroundings. Snacks of pork jelly, black pudding or bread and lard may accompany shots from the extensive range of vodkas (house Starka also available). Those with larger appetites can opt for a hefty mixed grill, trout or a tasty roast duck breast salad with grapes and raspberry vinaigrette. Krakow-style baked potatoes come with each dish. Caricatures from turn-of-the-century Berlin line the walls. *Ul.Józefa 14.* ☎ *012-430-65-38. Entrees 22–59zł. AE, DC, MC, V. Lunch & dinner daily. Map p 100.*

Szara OLD TOWN *POLISH/INTERNATIONAL* One of the most famous places in town, with a sister branch in Kazimierz, 'Gray' provides a constant turnover of tourists with hefty portions of duck, veal and beef

Trzy Papryczki for fantastic pizzas and imaginative veggie options.

lavished with wine or fruit sauces. Specialties include the starter of smoked reindeer tartar with horseradish, porcini mushroom cream soup and a bouillabaisse available in two sizes. All is very formal, set in a vaulted townhouse rebuilt in the 18th century, but there's also a separate bar if you're just after a drink and a bite on the market square. *Rynek Główny 6.* ☎ *012-421-66-69. Entrees 29–83zł. AE, DC, MC, V. Lunch & dinner daily. Map p 99.*

Trzy Papryczki OLD TOWN *PIZZAS* Commonly acknowledged to dish up the best pizzas in town, the Three Peppers uses all kinds of ingredients to flavor their famous pies. All come in two sizes and priced in the 19–40zł. range. The signature three peppers variety comes with mild or spicy salami, the vegetarian features fennel, aubergine and broccoli, while the most unusual comprises roast turkey, almonds and avocado. There are soups, salads, pastas and meat dishes, as well as imaginative vegetarian dishes—aubergine filled with spinach and tomato, for example. The affordable house wine comes from Puglia. *Ul.Poselski 17.*

☎ *012-292-55-32.*
AE, DC, MC, V. Lunch & dinner daily.
Map p 99.

Vega NEAR OLD TOWN VEGETAR-
IAN   As Krakow's prime meat-free
restaurant, Vega takes its mission
seriously. Each of its two branches—
this relaxed one has a terrace by the
Mehoffer Museum in the University
Quarter—displays a large spread of
salads, behind which a board shows
the half-dozen suggestions for a
main dish. Stuffed peppers, pancakes or pierogi, nothing will cost
more than 10zł. Salads are sold in
two sizes, and can be accompanied
by over 30 types of teas—there are
little fruit cocktails too. Vergnano
coffee is a welcome rare find in
these parts. A winter fireplace adds
a homely touch. *Ul.Krupnicza 22.*
☎ *012-430-08-46. Entrees 5–12.50zł.*
AE, DC, MC, V. Lunch & dinner daily.
Map p 99.

★★ Vinoteka La Bodega OLD
TOWN *SPANISH*   Wine bar, shop
and restaurant in one, this sleek
operation provides attractive
Mediterranean cuisine. No sloppy
microwaved meatballs here—tapas
come in the form of delicate *pintxos*
in two sizes, or sharing platters of
Spanish meats or cheeses. There
are hot appetizers too, fried *chis-
torra* sausage from Navarre, for
example, plus mains such as Spanish sirloin in three choices of sauce:
Gorgonzola, green pepper or
spinach. Wines are also mainly,
Spanish, with Enate from Aragon,
Erumir from Penedès and Nekeas
from Navarre. Many are sold at the
shop behind the dining room.
Ul.Sławkowska 12. ☎ *012-425-49-
81. AE, DC, MC, V. Lunch & dinner
daily. Map p 99.*

★★ Wentzl OLD TOWN *POLISH*
Beneath a sign dated 1792, this
gourmet fixture on the market

square is known for its signature
recipes, often game marinated in an
extravagant fruit-based sauce.
Examples include wild boar tender-
loin with dried cranberries in honey
liqueur and roast garlic sauce, and
stewed rabbit in horseradish sauce
with apple-scented beetroots. You'll
also find saddle of venison marinated in lemongrass with aromatic
cinnamon bark and redcurrant
sauce. Curiosities among the soups
and starters include mosaic of shark
in Parma ham with citrus sauce, and
cappuccino cream of artichoke. All
is served beneath timber beams in
heritage surroundings. *Rynek
Glówny 19.* ☎ *012-429-57-12.*
*Entrees 39–75zł. AE, DC, MC, V.
Lunch from 1pm & dinner daily. Map
p 99.*

Youmiko Sushi Bar OLD TOWN
JAPANESE   The newest of 10 sushi
venues around Krakow, this one goes
to show that good things really do
come in small packages. In a diminu-
tive room in minimalist style, delicate
shapes of rice, fish and vegetables
are created to order, half the fun
being watching the expert chef prepare your hosomaki, futomaki or
nigiri. Varieties run from a basic
cucumber hosomaki to an unagi of
grilled eel, omelet and asparagus.
Ul.Szczepański 7. ☎ *012-421-26-99.*
*Entrees 8–29zł. AE, DC, MC, V. Lunch
& dinner daily. Map p 99.*

Zapiecek Polskie Pierogarnie
OLD TOWN *POLISH*   Another local
Old Town cheapie, this pierogi place
dishes out steaming bowls of
dumplings from a little hatch.
Zapiecek is anything but sloppy
though—the wooden interior is kept
clean, the pierogi (sweet or savory)
prepared to traditional recipes.
Ul.Sławkowska 32. ☎ *012-422-74-
95. Entrees 8–17zł. No credit cards.
Lunch & dinner until 9pm daily. Map
p 99.* ●

Nightlife Best Bets

Best Bar For Music
★ B-Side *Ul.Estery 16* (p 115)

Best Microbrewery
★ C.K.Browar *Ul.Podwale 6-7* (p 115)

Best Gay Entertainment
★★★ Klub Cocon *Ul.Gazowa 21* (p 120)

Best Impersonation of a Classic Parisian Bar
★★★ Les Couleurs *Ul.Estery 10* (p 115)

Best Summer Terraces
Mleczarnia *Ul.Meiselsa 20* (p 117); Cudowne Lata *Ul.Karmelicza 43* (p 115)

Best Classic Cocktails
★★★ Paparazzi *Ul.Mikolajska 9* (p 117); ★★★ M Club *Ul.Św.Tomasza 11a* (p 119)

Best Retro Style
★★★ Łubu Dubu *Ul.Wielopole 15* (p 119); ★ Czetery Pokoje *Ul.Gołębie 6* (p 116)

Best Theme Bar
★★★ Propaganda *Ul.Miodowa 20* (p 117)

Best River View
★★★ Drukarnia *Ul.Nadwiślańska 1* (p 116)

Best Female-Friendly Bar
Miejsce *Ul.Estery 1* (p 116)

Best Irish Pub
★ Nic Nowego *Ul.Św.Krzyża 15* (p 117)

Best Atmosphere
★★★ Piękny Pies *Ul.Sławkowska 6a* (p 119); ★★★ Singer *Ul.Estery 20* (p 118)

Best Gay/Straight Mix
★★★ Kitsch *Ul.Wielopole 15* (p 120)

Best Grungy Basement
★ Roentgen *Pl.Szczepański 3* (p 120)

Best Quality DJs
★ Cień *Ul.Św.Jana 15* (p 118); ★ Rdza *Ul.Bracka 3-5* (p 120); ★★ Kijow Club *Al.Krasińskiego 34* (p 119)

Best Bar Chatter
★★ Dym *Ul.Św.Tomasza 13* (p 116)

★ Migrena *Ul.Gołębie 3* (p 116)

Best Mindless Fun
★ Afera *Ul.Sławkowska 13-15* (p 118)

Best Female-Friendly Bar: Miejsce.

Central Nightlife

1. Afera
2. Awaria
3. Black Gallery
4. Boom Bar Rush
5. C.K. Browar
6. Cień
7. Cudowne Lata
8. Cztery Pokoje
9. Dym
10. Enso
11. Kijów Club
12. Kitsch
13. Lubu Dubu
14. M Club
15. Migrena
16. Młoda Nowa Polska
17. Music Bar 9/ Light Box Gallery
18. Nic Nowego
19. Paparazzi
20. Pauza
21. Piękny Pies
22. Playground
23. Rdza
24. Roentgen

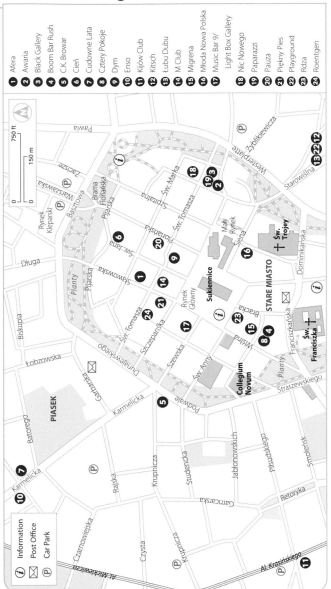

Information
Post Office
Car Park

Kazimierz & Podgórze Nightlife

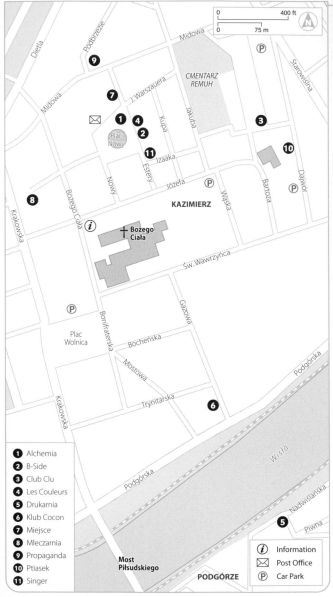

1 Alchemia
2 B-Side
3 Club Clu
4 Les Couleurs
5 Drukarnia
6 Klub Cocon
7 Miejsce
8 Mleczarnia
9 Propaganda
10 Ptiasek
11 Singer

ⓘ Information
✉ Post Office
Ⓟ Car Park

Krakow Nightlife A to Z

Bars and Pubs

★★ **Alchemia** KAZIMIERZ The bar that started the Kazimierz craze, Alchemia can still shake a thing or two—it'll be packed to the gills most weekends until 4am. A long, scuffed wooden interior is entered via the bar area, where drinks must be ordered and picked up. In summer, grab an outdoor table at this busy corner of Plac Nowy before the crowds get here. *Ul.Estery 5.* ☎ *012-421-22-00. Map p 114.*

★ **B-Side** KAZIMIERZ This small, neat bar on Plac Nowy is where music lovers tend to drift to—note the stills from the Joy Division film *Closer* and lampshades with portraits of rock stars on them. There's a nice buzz around the tiny bar counter, with conspiratorial talk over a few tall beers. *Ul.Estery 16.* ☎ *0694-46-14-03. Map p 114.*

Black Gallery OLD TOWN Back in the 1990s, the Old Town was full of smoky cellars filled with students getting wasted on cheap shots. The Black Gallery is the last of a dying breed, as these bars have become trendified or turned into DJ spots. It is set on three levels, linked by an industrial-looking staircase, down which stagger Goths, beatniks and assorted crazies. Most chase shots with big beers, while the occasional foreigner might order up a fearsomely strong cocktail. *Ul.Mikoljska 24.* ☎ *012-423-00-30. Map p 113.*

★ **C.K. Browar** NEAR OLD TOWN Krakow's main microbrewery bar is a commendably rowdy affair, groups of local lads laying into the house ale by the chunky glassful. The brews, concocted in massive copper vats, include dark, wheat and ginger varieties. There's food too, CK platters of ribs, chops and cutlets.

Those hiring the Hunting Room should prepare themselves for roast boar, ostrich or venison in mushroom sauce. DJs spin at weekends and football games are shown on big screens. *Ul.Podwale 6-7.* ☎ *012-429-25-05. Map p 113.*

★★★ **Les Couleurs** KAZIMIERZ Probably the best bar on Plac Nowy, Colors is a French-style café with an imposing zinc bar counter, banquettes and pleasing touches of Francophilia—old theatre posters, Serge Gainsbourg paraphernalia and a big bottle of Pernod behind the bar. By day, regulars enjoy breakfast and check their emails. By the evening, customers shed their novels and newspapers, beers flow and the chat gets loud. Open until 2am at weekends, Les Couleurs is as lively as the best of them. *Ul.Estery 10.* ☎ *012-429-42-70. Map p 114.*

★ **Cudowne Lata** NEAR OLD TOWN The slowly burgeoning University Quarter is becoming the place to be—as proven by the popularity of this student-friendly garden

French style café Les Couleurs.

bar occupying the ground floor of a big old house. The Wonder Years appeals to the kind of person happy with a dark Żywiec in front of them, and not fussed if there are holes in the table doileys. A lively musical backdrop is piped out to the fenced-in front garden in summer. *Ul.Karmelicka 43.* ☎ *012-632-27-29. Map p 113.*

★ **Cztery Pokoje** OLD TOWN Four Rooms is one of the best options for late-night fun in the Old Town. Four areas decorated with retro swirls and shapes are filled with pretty young things sucking beer through a straw or hitting the bright Kamikaze shots. Well-chosen music plays throughout and this is as good a place as anywhere to try out the local barman's cocktail-mixing skills—a Mojito will set you back 114ł. *Ul.Gołębie 6.* ☎ *012-421-10-14. Map p 113.*

★★★ **Drukarnia** PODGÓRZE The move of the legendary Drukarnia bar from Kazimierz to Podgórze in 2007 signaled a major shift in Krakow's geographical hierarchy—before that no one would have had any reason to cross the river. Now this laid-back, waterfront café fills every day from lunchtime, regulars spilling over from the shabby main bar and extensive new back room onto the pavement outside. It's also a jazz venue, with occasional concerts, but most come here for beer, gossip and the bohemian atmosphere. *Ul.Nadwiślańska 1.* ☎ *012-656-65-60. Map p 114.*

★★ **Dym** OLD TOWN Of the cluster of venues touching terraces in this quiet little courtyard corner of the Old Town, Dym attracts the most barflies. They gather along the narrow bar counter or at a table in the equally modest front room, filling the air with chatter and *dym* (smoke) until midnight. After that everyone, including the bar staff, staggers off to Piękny Pies. *Ul.Św.Tomasza 13.* ☎ *012-429-66-61. Map p 113.*

★★ **Miejsce** KAZIMIERZ Probably the most female-friendly of the Plac Nowy bars, this bare, retro venue rarely attracts idiots on stag nights—the grey door is too obscurely signposted to drag them in. Inside, a vintage TV, Commie-era film posters and a few strange lamps surround an intelligent, young crowd, intent on discussing culture and the issues of the day rather than diving into wanton hedonism. *Ul.Estery 1.* ☎ *0783-09-60-16. Map p 114.*

★ **Migrena** OLD TOWN Two bars stand side-by-side here: one named after the house address itself, and this one named after a particularly bad headache. Both are small, arty and bohemian in style, and filled with sturdy wooden furniture—Migrena stands out because of the impressive model of Krakow crowning its bar counter. Both make a handy pit stop on any Old Town bar crawl—especially if you're bound for Cztery Pokoje across the street. *Ul.Gołębie 3.* ☎ *012-430-24-18. Map p 113.*

Retro venue Miejsce.

★★ **Mleczarnia** KAZIMIERZ

Krakow's only real beer terrace is set at one end of the famous courtyard Spielberg shot in 'Schindler's List'—a relaxing and historic location. Across Meiselsa is Mleczarnia's other spot, a tiny bar filled with bric-a-brac, its doorway open on to the street. This is Krakow at its most bohemian, obscure, random and irresistible. *Ul.Meiselsa 20.* ☎ *012-421-85-32. Map p 114.*

★ **Młoda Nowa Polska** OLD

TOWN   This underrated music bar stands close to the Maly Rynek, three rooms with walls covered in newspaper articles. It looks like it would be more at home in Kazimierz, except for the big TV for football, darts machine and tap of Murphy's, attracting a handful of expats to join the young, local crowd. A good choice of music is another key factor. *Ul.Stolarska 1.* ☎ *012-422-29-49. Map p 113.*

★ **Nic Nowego** OLD TOWN   The

best of Krakow's Irish bars is a cut above—the contemporary décor, the retro local photography and the laudable policy of refusing stag parties. A range of quality spirits stands behind the bar—vodkas, gins, whiskies— near the tap providing the best Guinness in town. A large screen beams Sky Sports TV, packing in punters three deep at the narrow bar counter. *Ul.Św.Krzyża 15.* ☎ *012-421-61-88. Map p 113.*

★★★ **Paparazzi** OLD TOWN

The self-styled top cocktail spot in town, with similar branches in Warsaw, Łodź and Wrocław, Paparazzi exudes an image of cool class with its framed black-and-white photos of Hollywood stars, constant beaming of Fashion TV and extensive drinks list. Neither snobby nor exclusive, Paparazzi simply purveys proper mixed drinks to an appreciative clientele—prices are not significantly

The bohemian Mleczarnia.

higher than elsewhere in the Old Town. Imaginative domestic touches feature prominently—the Polish Martini of Absolut, Żubrówka and Krupnik, the Kraków variety with Absolut, Wiśniówka and fresh grapefruit. There is food too, baguettes, burgers and pastas. *Ul.Mikolajska 9.* ☎ *012-429-45-97. Map p 113.*

★★★ **Propaganda** KAZIMIERZ

Although it's a well-worn concept, this hard-drinking, Communist-themed, Kazimierz bar wears it well. People (mainly locals) don't come here to gawp and coo at the old signage, machines and banners, they plot up around the crowded wooden interior to banter loudly and drink their faces off. A musical soundtrack of indie, punk and metal attracts a mainly (but not exclusively) male clientele, who somehow keep the party going to shortly before the trams start running. *Ul.Miodowa 20.* ☎ *012-292-04-02. Map p 114.*

★★ **Ptiasek** KAZIMIERZ   Set away

from the Plac Nowy action, the Bird is the perfect spot to read, check emails or play chess by day, or enjoy a couple of quiet ones to start the evening off. Taps of Guinness, Tyskie and Pilsner Urquell are provided for tranquil sipping, with little squares of apple cake for something to nibble on. There's a garden in summer. *Ul.Dajwór 3.* ☎ *012-431-03-41. Map p 114.*

★★★ **Singer** KAZIMIERZ There's a strong case for naming Singer the best bar in Krakow—and on its night, way past midnight, it can be. Drinkers gather around tables made from old sewing machines in two dimly-lit rooms to create an atmosphere of conspiratorial chatter. The drink of choice is not beer—although you might spot a few stray stags chugging away—but Wiśniówka, the sticky cherry-flavored vodka that the barman will magically produce from behind a secret curtain. In summer, customers gather on the pavement to transform Plac Nowy into something continental and sophisticated. *Ul.Estery 20.* ☎ *012-292-06-22. Map p 114.*

Clubs

★ **Afera** OLD TOWN At this unashamed pick-up joint, local girls staggering down the precarious staircase in high heels to fish out a man a couple of hours later. If you're just after a few drinks and a good time, the cavernous, bare-brick Afera can deliver that too, with plenty of dancing to the regular in-house DJs spinning mainstream tunes. *Ul.Sławkowska 13-15.* ☎ *012-421-17-71. Closed Mon. Map p 113.*

Awaria OLD TOWN A varied agenda of DJs and live acts keeps the regulars entertained at this good-time cellar venue. Under the slogan 'Enough Is Never Enough', locals and expats sink standard beers, cocktails and vodka shots around a bar decked out in Americana. Mistletoe hanging over the counter causes a few giggles. *Ul.Mikolajska 9.* ☎ *012-292-03-50. Map p 113.*

★ **Boom Bar Rush.** OLD TOWN In the same building as Cztery Pokoje, BBR is an intimate, late-opening cellar club, the perfect last stop before bed. Regular DJs spin R&B and hip hop six nights of the week, theme nights as well, though room to dance is in pretty short supply. *Ul.Gołębia 6.* ☎ *012-429-39-74. Closed Mon. Map p 113.*

★ **Cień** OLD TOWN The red-lit cellar is perhaps Krakow's best nightspot for house DJs. The Shadow attracts a fashionable young crowd—there's no dress code but hair gel helps—who enjoy the constant crush between the bare-brick walls. Look hard and you'll find an intimate corner somewhere among the vaults. *Ul.Św.Jana 15.* ☎ *012-422-21-77. Map p 113.*

★ **Club Clu** KAZIMIERZ On tourist-swamped Szeroka, lined with terrace restaurants, Club Clu is a tidy late-night spot for dancers and lounge lizards. A complete mix of music is played until 5am at weekends, causing occasional wild gyration in the bare-brick space dimly illuminated by gas lamps. It's a bar as well—you can hire a table—so you can take it easy if so required. *Ul.Szeroka 10. 012-429-26-09. Closed Sun. Map p 114.*

★★ **Enso** NEAR OLD TOWN Cocktail bar, restaurant and nightclub in one, Enso's is the key venue in this quietly happening stretch of the University Quarter. The DJ action takes place in the weekend-only cellar, chic grown-ups mingling over well mixed cocktails while a decent DJ makes full use of Krakow's finest sound system. Upstairs, pick from 40 mixed drinks and perch on one of the spring stools around a small bar counter. Risottos, salads and pastas are served to a professional crowd by day. *Ul.Karmelicka 52.* ☎ *012-633-65-20. Map p 113.*

★★ Kijów Club NEAR OLD TOWN
Cross the lobby of the Kijów cinema
to find the door leading down to this
minimalist basement club. Decent
drinks at regular prices are served
from the green-lit bar while a DJ spins
electro tunes. Visuals appear on a
big screen and little TV screens in the
floor and everything is made to look
as if the space is three times bigger
than it actually is. Well respected
around town for the quality of its
spinning. *Al.Krasińskiego 34.* ☎ *012-
433-00-33. Closed Tue. Map p 113.*

★★★ Łubu Dubu NEAR OLD TOWN
Wielopole 15, near the Holiday Inn, is
a building completely given over to
party. Bars line each floor, allowing
you to hop from one to the other. This
one is often the best. Amid retro
kitsch, bar staff and regulars buy each
other drinks to a completely eclectic
soundtrack, everyone who can't fit
around the narrow bar area gathering
in the spaces at each end—dancing
might break out in one. *Ul.Wielopole
15.* ☎ *0694-46-14-02. Map p 113.*

★★★ M Club OLD TOWN   The
classiest of the Old Town's late-night
cellars, the M Club mixes quality
cocktails (toasted almond martinis,
proper mimosas) to well dressed
grown-ups over a soundtrack of
Latin and electro beats. This is
where young professionals come to

Cocktails, dinner and dancing at Enso.

mingle. Everything is either red-lit or
glass-topped, and if you're not sleek,
you don't fit in. *Ul.Św.Tomasza 11a.*
☎ *012-431-00-49. Closed Sun, Mon,
Tue. Map p 113.*

**★ Music Bar 9/Light Box
Gallery** OLD TOWN   The most popular place on the Szewska bar strip is
in fact two places in one: above, the
Light Box Gallery is a busy, pleasant
bar with enough space to allow the
odd game of darts. Downstairs is a
sweaty cellar with a commercial
soundtrack and alcoves to get to
know your newly found friend a little
better. In summer, a courtyard
comes into its own. *Ul.Szewska 9.*
☎ *012-422-25-46. Map p 113.*

★★★ Pauza OLD TOWN   Pauza is
really two venues in one. Downstairs
is a labyrinthine cellar, no different
to any other in this part of the Old
Town. One floor up, though, is one
of Krakow's best nightspots, a big
bar with arty touches, a sassy staff
and plenty of room to move. There
are exhibitions and films shown too,
attracting an intelligent crowd a
world away from the drunken young
hordes hunting for casual compan-
ionship. *Ul.Floriańska 18/3.
www.pauza.pl. Map p 113.*

★★★ Piękny Pies OLD TOWN
The landmark Beautiful Dog, having
moved venues, can now accommodate at least three more people in
its main bar, busy back room and DJ
cellar. They could move it to the
Cloth Hall and still everyone would
want to be here—don't expect to
be served right away. People come
here to soak up a smoky mess of a
bar, and drink themselves senseless
without the slightest hint of embar-
rassment or stories the next day.
Downstairs the DJ keeps the crowd
frantically dancing to a complete
mix of tunes—rap, Motown, indie—
as people pour in from bars across
the city. *Ul.Sławkowska 6a.* ☎ *012-
421-45-52. Map p 113.*

Less Is More

For its multitude of late-night options, Krakow lacks the kind of massive superclubs you might find in other Polish cities or over the border in Germany. The upside of this is that many post-midnight options double up as both bar and club, with a modest dancefloor and no cover charge. If a venue has set a levy on the door—rarely over 10zł—it means that a half-decent DJ or band has been booked, and curiosity alone should merit forking out the modest admission.

★ **Playground** NEAR OLD TOWN The unique Wielopole 15 is a maze of bars and clubs set within one open building—this spot, on a lower floor, spins indie, reggae, rap, soul, anything to keep the crowd happy and sinking the beers here and not any place else. *Ul.Wielopole 15.* ☎ *0600-31-16-59. Map p 113.*

★ **Rdza** OLD TOWN Rust is probably the best of a lively cluster of bars and clubs at this junction of Bracka and the main market square. A dark cellar accessed via a spiral staircase accommodates some of the best local house DJs in the business. There are enough alternatives within a five-minute radius if it all gets a bit claustrophobic around the modest dancefloor *Ul.Bracka 3-5.* ☎ *0600-39-55-41. Closed Sun, Mon Tue. Map p 113.*

Kitsch décor and an eclectic playlist at Łubu Dubu.

★ **Roentgen** OLD TOWN As dark a basement as you'll find in Krakow— which is saying something—the X-Ray pounds out ear-splitting techno and punk sounds to a grungy crowd unperturbed by the lack of napkins or even chairs with cushions. It attracts a loyal crowd who've been coming here since the 1990s. *Pl.Szczepański 3.* ☎ *012-431-11-77. Map p 113.*

Gay-Friendly Venues

★★★ **Kitsch** NEAR OLD TOWN Occupying the top of the Wielopole 15 party building, Kitsch is a fantastically fun night out for gays and straights alike. Disco and dance tunes, long drinks and shots poured by a fun, with-it staff (two bar counters operate at weekends) and an up-for-it crowd make this one of Krakow's best nights out. Expect drag shows on busier nights. *Ul.Wielopole 15. www.kitsch.pl. Map p 113.*

★★★ **Klub Cocon** KAZIMIERZ As you gaze over the river from Podgórze, you can't fail to notice a wonderful commotion going on in a building on the opposite bank—that commotion is Klub Cocon. House and electro DJs, karaoke and occasional drag shows make this an essential stop on any Friday or Saturday night. There's plenty of room too—three bars, space on the dancefloor and intimacy in the alcoves and two dark rooms. *Ul.Gazowa 21.* ☎ *0501-35-06-65. www.klub-cocon.pl. Map p 114.* ●

Arts & Entertainment Best Bets

Best **Concert Acoustics**
★★★ Krakow Philharmonic
Ul.Zwierzyniecka 1 (p 125)

Best **Jazz Club**
★★★ U Muniaka *Ul.Floriańska 3
(p 128)*

Best **Opera House**
★★ Krakow Opera *Ul.Lubicz 48
(p 125)*

Best **Music Festival**
★★ Sacrum Profanum *various
venues (p 129)*

Best **Sports Entertainment**
★★ Wisła Kraków *Ul Reymonta 22
(p 129)*

Best **Theater Performances**
★★★ Stary Theater *Ul.Jagellońska
5l (p 130)*

Best **Theater Shows For Kids**
★★★ Groteska Theater *Ul.Skar-
bowa 2 (p 130)*

Best **All-Around Live Music
Venue**
★★ Showtime *Rynek Główny 28
(p 129)*

Best **Sweaty Jazz Cellar**
★★ Harris Piano Jazz Bar *Rynek
Główny 28 (p 127)*

Best **All-Around Performance
Venue**
★★★ Juliusz Słowacki Theater
Pl.Św.Ducha 1 (p 125)

Best **Classic Cinemas**
★★★ ARS Cinema *Ul.Św.Jana 6
(p 125)*; ★★★ Pod Baranami *Rynek
Główny 27 (p 126)*

Best **Big Movie Screens**
★ IMAX *Al.Pokoju 44 (p 126)*;
★★ Kijów *Ul.Krasińskiego 34 (p 126)*

Best **Grunge Den**
★★ Kawiarnia Naukowa *Ul.Jakuba
29-31 (p 128)*

Best **Eclectic Music Agenda**
★★ Rotunda *Ul.Oleandry 1 (p 128)*

Best **Art Gallery**
Bunkier Sztuki *Pl.Szczepański 3a
(p 127)*

Best Jazz Club: U Muniaka.

Old Town Arts & Entertainment

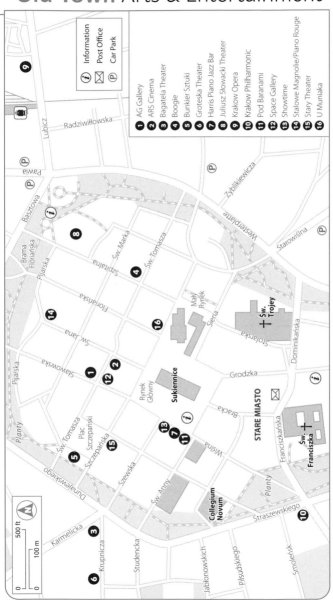

- (i) Information
- ✉ Post Office
- Ⓟ Car Park

1. AG Gallery
2. ARS Cinema
3. Bagatela Theater
4. Boogie
5. Bunkier Sztuki
6. Groteska Theater
7. Harris Piano Jazz Bar
8. Juliusz Slowacki Theater
9. Krakow Opera
10. Krakow Philharmonic
11. Pod Baranami
12. Space Gallery
13. Showtime
14. Stalowe Magnolie/Piano Rouge
15. Stary Theater
16. U Muniaka

Around Krakow A & E

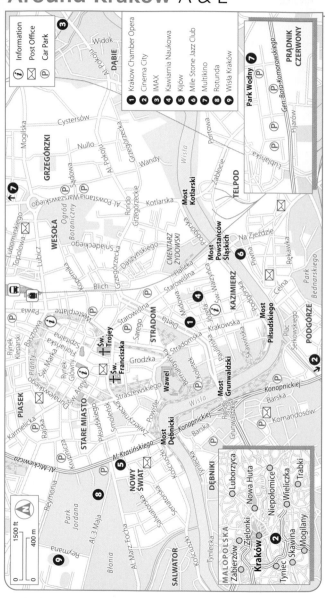

Legend:
- (i) Information
- ⊠ Post Office
- Ⓟ Car Park

1 Krakow Chamber Opera
2 Cinema City
3 IMAX
4 Kawiarnia Naukowa
5 Kijów
6 Mile Stone Jazz Club
7 Multikino
8 Rotunda
9 Wisła Kraków

Arts & Entertainment **A to Z**

Classical Music & Opera Venues

★★★ Juliusz Słowacki Theater

OLD TOWN   Krakow's most prestigious concert venue, an ornate confection at the northern end of Szpitalna dating from the 1890s, stages classical music, dance and theater productions. For 2007 and 2008, it has also been the home of Krakow Opera while its own venue is being prepared nearby on Ulica Lubicz. Here concert-goers can enjoy a pre-show drink at the stylish Café Trema downstairs. *Pl.Św.Ducha 1.* ☎ *012-424-45-00. www.slowacki. krakow.pl. Map p 123.*

★★ Krakow Chamber Opera

KAZIMIERZ   This intimate venue opened in 1991 thanks to actress and choreographer Jadwiga Leśniak-Jankowska. The Krakow Chamber Opera has been based here for most of the decade, its repertoire concentrating on old Polish traditional themes. *Ul.Miodowa 15.* ☎ *012-430-66-05. www.kok.art.pl. Map p 124.*

Juliusz Słowacki Theater.

★★ Krakow Opera NEAR OLD

TOWN   After a wait of five decades, Krakow Opera moves into a new, purpose-built venue in 2009. Construction of a new Opera House was agreed in 2002 and commenced in 2004. Meanwhile the company continued at venues around the city, most notably the Juliusz Słowacki Theater, the other side of the train station. By the summer of 2008, the opera management could confidently outline a program for the upcoming winter season—a première of Krzystof Penderecki's 'Ubu Roi' slated for December 2008. The new auditorium seats 760, with a 300 m^2 stage, a chamber stage, rehearsal rooms and, upstairs, a terrace restaurant and exhibition space. *Ul.Lubicz 48.* ☎ *012-296-61-00. www. opera.krakow.pl. Map p 123.*

★★★ Krakow Philharmonic

NOWY ŚWIAT   This impressive neo-baroque pile, built in 1931, became the home of the then newly formed Krakow Philharmonic in the last days of the war in 1945. Its main auditorium has hosted many top international names since a tradition to continue with the recent announcement of Tadeusz Strugała as general and artistic director. Strugała, artistic and chief conductor here in the 1980s, worked with Roman Polański on Oscar-winning film *The Pianist* in 2001. The Philharmonic also contains two rooms for chamber concerts. *Ul.Zwierzyniecka 1.* ☎ *012-422-94-77. www.opera.krakow.pl. Map p 123.*

Film

★★★ ARS Cinema OLD TOWN

The most elegant cinema in Krakow, set in two historic mansions a short walk from the main market square, comprises five screening rooms.

The 170-seater Reduta, a former ballroom, is the most impressive, while the Sztuki can accommodate more than 200. An adventurous agenda of European and arthouse works forms the bulk of the repertoire, while popular family-friendly films also get a look-in. *Ul.Św.Jana 6.* ☎ *012-421-41-99. www.ars.pl. Map p 123.*

★ **Cinema City** ŁAGIEWNIKI   Set on the main road leading south from the city centre an easy tram ride away, this 10-screen complex is the most comfortable venue to enjoy a movie in Krakow. Great for sound and special effects, Cinema City also scores high for accommodating wheelchair-bound moviegoers. *Ul.Zakopiańska 62.* ☎ *012-290-90-90. www.cinemacity.pl. Trams 8, 19, 22, 23, 40: Solvay. Map p 124.*

★ **IMAX** DĄBIE   Wildlife, sci-fi and adventure features are brought to life on a vast screen measuring 18 m by 22 m. The venue is an easy hop on the tram from town, heading towards Nowa Huta. *Al.Pokoju 44.* ☎ *012-290-90-90. www.kinoimax.pl. Trams 1, 14, 22: Kraków Plaza, Map p 124.*

★★ **Kijów** NOWY ŚWIAT   A major venue for the Krakow Film Festival, the contemporary Kijów can boast the largest cinema screen in central Krakow. As well as the 800-seater Large Hall, the Kijów also screens movies in an intimate studio space. The venue celebrated its 40th anniversary in 2007 by opening a basement DJ club accessed through the lobby. Excellent café-bar for pre- and post-film drinks. *Ul.Krasińskiego 34.* ☎ *012-433-00-33. www.kijow.pl. Map p 124.*

★ **Multikino** N.E. KRAKOW   This huge multiplex stands north of the city centre, conveniently right by the Aqua Park. A dozen screening rooms show mainly standard Hollywood

The contemporary Kijów cinema.

fare, with regular all-night themed marathons also programmed. Three bars include one especially for sports fans. *Ul.Dobrego Pasterza 128.* ☎ *012-617-63-99. www.kijow.pl. All buses to Dobrego Pasztorza. Map p 124.*

★★★ **Pod Baranami** OLD TOWN Right on the main market square, this palatial arena is one of the most famous cultural institutions in Krakow. The cinema comprises three screening rooms, Red, Blue and White, all with Dolby surround sound and air-conditioning, with a combined seating capacity of 250. Classic European and arthouse films are the order of the day. *Rynek Główny 27.* ☎ *012-423-07-68. www. kinopodbaranami.pl. Map p 123.*

Galleries
★★ **AG Gallery** OLD TOWN Many of Poland's most outstanding contemporary artists exhibit here, a large gallery a short walk from the main square. The in-house collection is constantly being added to, so there's usually something new each time you visit. *Ul.Sławkowski 10.* ☎ *012-429-51-78. www.galeriaag. art.pl. Map p 123.*

★★★ **Bunkier Sztuki** OLD TOWN This oddly attractive Modernist building on the Planty houses some of the city's best contemporary art exhibitions. As well as regular thought-provoking, mainly Polish shows, the Art Bunker hosts World Press Photo exhibition in the autumn. *Pl.Szczepański 3a.* ☎ *012-423-09-71. www.bunkier.com.pl. Map p 123.*

★★ **Space Gallery** OLD TOWN Filling a beautiful 16th-century townhouse on Floriańska, the Space Gallery begins at the 19th century (Matejko, the Paris School) and works its way up to regularly changing works of the modern day on the second floor. There's a sculpture section as well. *Ul.Floriańska 13.* ☎ *012-421-89-94. www.spacegallery. com.pl. Map p 123.*

Jazz & Cabaret

★ **Boogie** OLD TOWN Freshly renovated, this is one of Krakow's smartest places to catch live music and enjoy a cocktail. A regular agenda of quality acts performs in a light space decked out with large black-and-white photographs of jazz legends. Films are shown on Wednesdays and Sundays. *Ul.Szpitalna 9.* ☎ *012-429-43-06. www.boogiecafe. pl. Map p 123.*

★★ **Harris Piano Jazz Bar** OLD TOWN Right on the market square, this basement club is one of Krakow's most popular music venues. All the big names in Polish jazz have played here. The regular appearance of foreign guests and a flexible music policy—blues, R&B and folk—mean that Harris fills in summer and winter. Opening hours until 2am and a selection of 20 cocktails served from a long, busy bar counter keep the party going. *Rynek Główny 28.* ☎ *012-421-57-41. www. harris.krakow.pl. Map p 123.*

Mile Stone Jazz Club PODGÓRZE With its luxurious settees and low lighting, the Mile Stone on the ground floor of the Qubus business hotel is just the right place for a posh date—the discerning jazz fan is unlikely to find anything cutting-edge on stage here. A gentle agenda of swing and modern sounds is lined up for Fridays and Saturdays, with no cover charge. The riverside location lends a relaxing tone to the evening. *Ul.Nadwiślańska 6, Qubus Hotel.* ☎ *012-374-51-86. www.mile-stone. pl. Map p 124.*

★★★ **Stalowe Magnolie/Piano Rouge** OLD TOWN These two mainly jazz venues under the same management share a similar scarlet color scheme and louche style. The more recently opened Piano Rouge (Rynek Główny 46) sits on the main square—jazz piano sets suit the atmosphere perfectly. The Steel Magnolias has a long-established reputation hosting quality local jazz trios and solo singers. *Ul.Św.Jana*

Live music and cocktails at Boogie.

Harris Piano Jazz Bar.

15. ☎ 012-422-84-72. www.stalowe magnolie.com. Map p 123.

★★★ **U Muniaka** OLD TOWN *The* place for jazz in Krakow—for three nights a week at least. Founded by renowned saxophonist Janusz Muniak in 1992, this sturdy club set in a 16th-century townhouse close to the main square has hosted pretty much every name in Polish jazz. Muniak has also been able to attract the odd international

name too—Wynton Marsalis once jammed here. Concerts usually take place between Thursday and Saturday, although check the website for the weekly agenda. There's a full menu too, while beers and cocktails are set at standard prices. *Ul.Floriańska 3.* ☎ *012-423-12-05. www.umuniaka.krakow.pl. Map p 123.*

Pop & Rock

★★ **Kawiarnia Naukowa** KAZIMIERZ   Krakow's main grunge bar stages the occasional live act in cramped side room. Even if there's not a band on, then the vinyl spun behind the big stone bar is worth a visit to darkest Kazimierz—punk, Johnny Cash, Nirvana, whatever. Wonderfully friendly bar staff serves a loyal clientele. *Ul.Jakuba 29-31.* ☎ *0663-83-34-57.www.kawiarnia naukowa.ovh.org. Map p 124.*

★★ **Rotunda** CZARNA WIES Many a band has treaded the boards at this student centre venue near Park Jordan, a couple of tram stops from the Old Town. The booking policy is completely random— rock, rap, indie from home and abroad—but you might also find

Advance Tickets & Listings

For the latest concert, theater and event listings, pick up a copy of the monthly **moveout,** a guide to all entertainment in Krakow. It's available at bars and cafés around the city. Although it's written in Polish, the calendar section at the back is fairly easy to work out. The less conspicuous **megazine** performs a similar function. The more high-brow **Karnet** (monthly, Polish-English) and bi-monthly **events guide** are also widely available.

The people behind Karnet run an information bureau in town, the useful City Information Point (*Ul.2w.Jana 2,* ☎ *012-421-77-87, www.karnet.krakow.pl*). For tickets, your best bet is Empik (*Rynek Główny 5,* ☎ *012 423 81 90, www.empik.com*) on the main square.

Krakow Music Festivals

Krakow hosts so many festivals of classical music it's hard to keep track of them. Perhaps the most attractive is the fortnight-long **Music In Old Krakow** (☎ 012-421-45-66; www.capellacracoviensis. art.pl) every August, established by the early-music ensemble Capella Cracoviensis in 1976. Its main draw here is the range of concert venues—churches, chapels, squares, courtyards, college halls and most notably St Kinga's Chapel in the Wieliczka Salt Mine—and events tend to sell out quite quickly. September's **Sacrum Profanum** (www.sacrumprofanum.pl) has raised its profile and expanded its remit quite considerably. Focusing on 'sacred' and 'lay' music from one geographical region, to be performed in post-industrial spaces, for 2008's Germany special SP invited Kraftwerk to play three nights at the Nowa Huta complex and performers of Karlheinz Stockhausen at the Schindler Factory in Podgórze. For jazz, look out for July's **Summer Jazz Festival** (www.cracjazz.com), mainly in the Pod Baranami in the main market square. Kazimierz's **Jewish Cultural Festival** (www.jewishfestival.pl) in June always contains a strong (generally klezmer) musical element. The biggest mainsteam event is **Coke Live Music** over two days in August, at the Aviation Museum near Nowa Huta. Recent guests have included Jay-Z, Lily Allen and Faithless—for 2008, Timbaland, Missy Elliott and the Kaiser Chiefs were the headlining acts.

classical, spoken word or an evening with the local mountaineering society. *Ul.Oleandry 1.* ☎ *012-292-65-16. www.rotunda.pl. Trams 15, 18: Oleandry. Map p 124.*

★★ Showtime OLD TOWN   Right on the market square, this bohemian space hosts live music of all genres—anything that fits onto its modest stage in fact. One floor up, this is a rare Rynek Główny venue with a view of the square from above. Scale the carpeted staircase lined with bizarre decorations and see what's on that night. *Rynek Główny 28.* ☎ *012-421-47-14. Map p 123.*

Spectator Sports
★★ Wisła Kraków CZARNA WIES Poland's top football team in recent years play at the best league ground in the country. Despite this, and the city's palpably obvious talent for tourism, Krakow inexplicably remains on the reserve list for venues hosting the Euro 2012 championships. If someone sees sense, then this modern stadium by the Park Jordana will have its capacity doubled to 33,000. In the meantime, the home team plays every other weekend between August and May. Check the website for times—tickets can be bought on the day. Prestigious European games are an annual event—recent visitors have included Barcelona and Real Madrid. *Ul.Reymonta 22.* ☎ *012-630-76-00. www. wisla.krakow.pl. Trams 15, 18: Reymana n/ż. Map p 124.*

Theater

★★★ Bagatela Theater

NEAR OLD TOWN   Founded in 1919, the Bagatela occupies an impressive building where Karmelicka meets Krupnicza. Known for its light comedies and musicals, the Bagatela is also named after poet and literary professor Tadeusz Boy-Żeleński, murdered in the war. *Ul.Karmelicka 6.* ☎ *012-422-26-44. www. bagatela.pl. Map p 123.*

★★★ Groteska Theater NEAR OLD TOWN

Based at this remarkable building in the University Quarter since 1945, the Groteska also stages open-air puppet shows and re-enactments of Polish fairy tales in the main market square in summer. During the autumn-spring season, the Groteska produces mask and costumes dramas for children and adults, some veering on the experimental side. Children's workshops are also held. *Ul.Skarbowa 2.* ☎ *012-633-48-22. www.groteska.pl. Map p 123.*

★★★ Stary Theater OLD TOWN

Krakow's Old Theater has reflected the monumental changes in Polish history over its 200-plus years. Founded in 1781, and based at this building since 1799, the Stary had its heyday with the great names of the 19th century. Closed in the early 1900s, the Stary reopened immediately after the war, only for each subsequent director to come at loggerheads with the government censor. Much is documented in the modest museum downstairs, where you'll also find the Maska café, done out in the same art-nouveau style as the theater's façade. The Stary stages both Polish and international productions. *Ul.Jagellońska 5.* ☎ *012-422-85-66. www.stary-teatr. pl. Map p 123.* ●

Open-air puppet shows by the Groteska Theater.

Bagatela Theater for light comedy and musicals.

Lodging Best Bets

Best **Romantic Hotels**
★★★ Gródek $$$ *Ul.na Gródku 4 (p 139)*; ★★★ Amadeus $$$ *Ul.Mikolajska 20 (p 135)*

Best **Panoramic Pool**
★★★ Qubus Hotel $$$ *Ul.Nadwiślańska 6 (p 144)*

Best **Historic Conversions**
★★★ Copernicus $$$ *Ul.Kanonicza 16 (p 133)*; ★★★ Pugetów $$$ *Ul.Starowiślna 15a (p 143)*; ★★★ Stary $$$ *Ul.Szczepańska 5 (p 145)*

Best **Riverside Views**
★ Poleski $$ *Ul.Sandomierska 6 (p 142)*

Best **Art-Nouveau Decor**
★ Pollera $$ *Ul.Szpitalna 30 (p 143)*

Best **Main Market Square Locations**
★★★ Wentzl $$$ *Rynek Główny 19 (p 146)*; ★★★ Pałac Bonerowski $$$ *Ul.Św.Jana 1 (p 142)*; ★ Dom Polonii $ *Rynek Główny 14 (p 137)*

Best **Surprising Attractions**
★★ Eden $$ *Ul.Ciemna 15 (p 137)*

Best **Spa Hotel**
★★★ Farmona Business Hotet and Spa $$$ *Ul.Jugowicka 10c (p 138)*

Best **Backpacker Hostel**
★★ Flamingo $ *Ul.Szewska 4 (p 138)*

Best **Film-Set Location**
★★★ Grand Hotel $$$ *Ul.Sławkowska 5-7 (p 139)*

Best **Bed and Breakfast**
★★ Kolory Bed and Breakfast $ *Ul.Estery 10 (p 140)*

Best **Kazimierz Lodging**
★★ Rubinstein $$$ *Ul.Szeroka 12 (p 145)*

Best for **Families**
★ Novotel Centrum $$ *Ul.Kościuszki 5 (p 141)*

Best for **Visiting Wawel**
★ Pod Wawelem $$ *Pl.Na Groblach 22a (p 142)*; ★★ Sheraton Kraków $$$ *Ul. Powiśle 7 (p 145)*

Best **Blueprint** for **Success**
★ Art Hotel Niebieski $$ *Ul.Flisacka 3 (p 135)*

Wentzl, one of the best market square locations.

Old Town Lodging

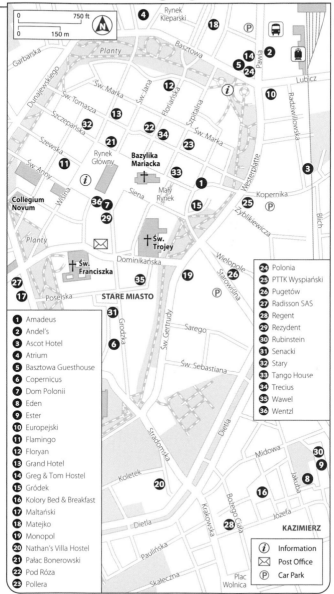

1 Amadeus
2 Andel's
3 Ascot Hotel
4 Atrium
5 Basztowa Guesthouse
6 Copernicus
7 Dom Polonii
8 Eden
9 Ester
10 Europejski
11 Flamingo
12 Floryan
13 Grand Hotel
14 Greg & Tom Hostel
15 Gródek
16 Kolory Bed & Breakfast
17 Maltański
18 Matejko
19 Monopol
20 Nathan's Villa Hostel
21 Pałac Bonerowski
22 Pod Róza
23 Pollera

24 Polonia
25 PTTK Wyspiański
26 Pugetów
27 Radisson SAS
28 Regent
29 Rezydent
30 Rubinstein
31 Senacki
32 Stary
33 Tango House
34 Trecius
35 Wawel
36 Wentzl

i Information
✉ Post Office
Ⓟ Car Park

Kazimierz & Podgórze Lodging

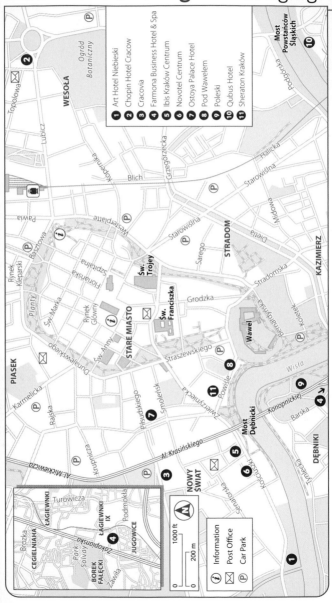

1 Art Hotel Niebieski
2 Chopin Hotel Cracow
3 Cracovia
4 Farmona Business Hotel & Spa
5 Ibis Kraków Centrum
6 Novotel Centrum
7 Ostoya Palace Hotel
8 Pod Wawelem
9 Poleski
10 Qubus Hotel
11 Sheraton Kraków

Information
Post Office
Car Park

1000 ft
200 m

Krakow Lodging **A to Z**

★★★ Amadeus OLD TOWN   This converted 16th-century townhouse is one of Krakow's most opulent hotels, popular with visiting writers and classical pianists. The title refers to the baroque style of the rooms and public spaces, including the cellar restaurant and café, purveyor of delicate little cakes. Amid all this chintz, the service is first-class, befitting Amadeus' four-star status. *Ul.Mikolajska 20. ☎ 012-429-60-70. www.hotel-amadeus.pl. 22 units. Doubles 470–650zł. AE, DC, MC, V. Map p 133.*

★★ Andel's NEAR OLD TOWN Dominating the landscaped square by the train station, this sleek business hotel allows for a comfortable, quiet, high-tech stay near the Old Town and market square. Flat-screen TVs, high-speed internet and underfloor heated bathrooms feature throughout, with a gym, sauna and massage treatments also available. Guests mingle in Oscar's Bar (brunch, jazz, cocktails) and the Delight restaurant with its summer terrace. Rates vary—look out for special offers. *Ul.Pawia 1. ☎ 012-660-01-00. www.andelscracow.com. 159 units. Doubles 400–760zł. AE, DC, MC, V. Map p 133.*

★ Art Hotel Niebieski SALWA-TOR   Having awarded itself three-and-a-half star status, the management is going the whole hog in 2009, adding 30 rooms, a spa, underground parking, panoramic restaurant, conference area and four-star tag by 2010. It's a wise gamble—serene Salwator is where moneyed locals are setting up home, near town and towards the airport. For the moment, the Niebieksi, overlooking the river near the tram terminus, justifies its rating with floor-heated

Sleek business hotel Andels.

bathrooms, individual internet access and, in Il Fresco, a decent restaurant. *Ul.Flisacka 3. ☎ 012-431-18-58. www.niebieski.com.pl. 13 units. Doubles 290–380zł. AE, DC, MC, V. Map p 134.*

Ascot Hotel NEAR OLD TOWN Opened in 2007, near the main train station east of the Old Town, this modern, comfortable three-star is a handy mid-range option close to the action. Free wireless Internet comes in all rooms along with a white orange and pastel color scheme, also used in the public spaces as well—both bar and restaurant have a contemporary feel. Discounts are offered for three-night weekend stays. *Ul.Radwiła łowska 3. ☎ 012-384-06-06. www.ascothotel.pl. 49 units. Doubles 290–390zł. AE, DC, MC, V. Map p 133.*

The Best Lodging

★ **Atrium** NEAR OLD TOWN   Only a three-star this, but perfectly comfortable, and set in a quiet location north of the Old Town near Kleparz market. The neat rooms and restaurant exude light and space, all equipped with modern furnishings and ably manned by a polite staff. Discounts are offered on room rates and meals in summer. *Ul.Krzywa 7.* ☎ *012-430-02-03. www.hotelatrium. com.pl. 50 units. Doubles 290–390zł. AE, DC, MC, V. Map p 133.*

★ **Basztowa Guesthouse** NEAR OLD TOWN   A centrally located bargain this, a hop from the main train station and the Old Town nearby. Rooms with their own shower are nearly twice the price of those without—these showers being narrow and cramped, the outlay is hardly worth it. No complaints with the rest of the furnishings, the style of this 19th-century townhouse brought out by the carved woods and parquet floors. Pick up your keys from the Hotel Polonia next door. *Ul.Basztowa 24.* ☎ *012-429-51-81. www.hotelsinkrakow.pl. 24 units. Doubles 109–195zł. AE, DC, MC, V. Map p 133.*

★ **Chopin Hotel Cracow** GRZE-GORZKI   Three-star sister of the Andel's, the Chopin is equally bright and breezy if perhaps a tad more functional than its more prestigious relation. Stuck out just east of the Old Town, a couple of tram stops away, it offers guests just enough (bar, restaurant, gym, massage treatments, beauty salon, summer garden) that a hop to town need not be necessary if time is tight. All rooms have free high-speed WiFi too. *Ul.Przy Rondzie 2.* ☎ *012-299-00-00. www.chopinhotel.pl. 220 units. Doubles 266–364zł. AE, DC, MC, V. Map p 134.*

★★★ **Copernicus** OLD TOWN   Candidate for best lodging in town, Poland's only Relais & Châteaux hotel has hosted British royals, American presidents and Saudi dignitaries. Both historic (it's an early 16th-century conversion) and contemporary (high-speed WiFi in each room, high-tech conference room in the Fireplace Hall), the Copernicus offers a roof-top terrace in full view of Wawel Castle. Designers have, somehow, arranged a swimming pool, gym and sauna in the medieval cellars. The sumptuous furnishings fit the surroundings, and the restaurant is one of Krakow's finest. *Ul.Kanonicza 16.* ☎ *012-424-34-00. www.hotel.com.pl. 29 units. Doubles 650–980zł. AE, DC, MC, V. Map p 133.*

Art Hotel Niebieski.

★ **Cracovia** NEAR OLD TOWN
Everyone knows the Cracovia. A
behemoth occupying the prominent
junction where the city center ends
and the Błonia Meadow begins,
handy for the National Museum and
football grounds, the Cracovia is the
setting-off point for tourist buses to
Auschwitz, Wieliczka and beyond.
The rooms are pretty functional but
improved of late, with internet
access and direct-dial international
telephone lines. Although not
included in the price—what do you
expect for 200zł—the Cracovia can
organize canoeing, horse-riding,
tennis, cycling and swimming at an
outdoor pool. *Al.Focha 1.* ☎ *012-
424-56-00. www.orbisonline.pl. 314
units. Doubles 290–560zł. AE, DC,
MC, V. Map p 134.*

Dom Polonii OLD TOWN Book
well in advance for the best-located
rooms in town—all three of them,
overlooking the market square from
their vantage point on the third floor
of this historic townhouse. There's
no lift but the units are big enough
to accommodate a bathtub and the
high ceilings more than make up for
any lack of space. *Rynek Główny 14.*
☎ *012-428-04-60. www.wspolnota-
polska.krakow.pl. 3 units. Doubles
237zł. AE, DC, MC, V. Map p 133.*

★★ **Eden** KAZIMIERZ This otherwise modest three-star in the Jewish
quarter hides a surprising array of
unusual facilities, most notably the
only authentic mikvah bath in town.
The other unexpected feature is a salt
grotto, while a sauna and massage
are also available on-site. All these
attractions are paid extras—the mikvah is open to non-guests—but
ensure that this pretty, decorative
mid-range trove is busy all year
round. Also to hand are a genuinely
kosher restaurant and Ye Olde Goat
sports bar, in a historic part of a building once occupied by Isaac Jakubow-
icz, founder of the nearby synagogue

*Copernicus, the hotel favoured by visiting
royals and presidents.*

of the same name. *Ul.Ciemna 15.*
☎ *012-430-65-65. www.hoteleden.pl.
27 units. Doubles 280–380zł. AE, DC,
MC, V. Map p 133.*

★ **Ester** KAZIMIERZ Probably the
most expensive three-star in town,
but you're paying for the location
and the view over the Jewish hub of
Szeroka. The other key attraction is
the range of massages available—
Polynesian, aromatherapy, anti-
stress—attracting a constant traffic
of business custom. Given the room
rates, the restaurant is reasonably
priced, with dishes kosher and non-.
Ul.Szeroka 20. ☎ *012-429-11-68.
www.hotel-ester.krakow.pl. 32 units.
Doubles 170–379zł. AE, DC, MC, V.
Map p 133.*

Europejski NEAR OLD TOWN
Don't be put off by the retro blue
neon sign blinking away as you exit
the train station—this former state-
run flophouse has been completely
overhauled and provides a comfortable mid-range stay within easy
reach of all downtown amenities.
Behind this transformation is Jacek
Czepczyk, now able to invest his
time and money into improving this
homely, family-run hostelry, its Kos-
sakówa restaurant and Noblesse bar.

Flamingo Hostel for a great base in the Old Town.

Ul.Lubicz 5. ☎ *012-423-25-10. www. he.pl. 48 units. Doubles 355–455zł. AE, DC, MC, V. Map p 133.*

★★★ Farmona Business Hotel & Spa ŁAGIEWNIKI

This wonderful leafy retreat is worth the hassle of its out-of-town location—build a relaxing weekend around it. Opened in 2006, set in an extensive garden with gazebo, the Farmona provides the finest spa treatments in Krakow and the best hotel breakfast, served on the terrace of the Restaurant Magnifica, whose fusion cuisine warrants an evening here alone. Guests lie around the Oriental-style spa area, drifting out to the sound of running water. The steam room and dry sauna (watch out for the weird jungle sounds) can be enjoyed with a range of creams and treatments. *Ul.Jugowicka 10c.* ☎ *012-252-70-70. www.farmonahotel. com. 31 units. Doubles 400–430zł. AE, DC, MC, V. Map p 134.*

★★ Flamingo OLD TOWN

There are currently a hundred hostels in Krakow—when this superior one set up a couple of years ago near the main square, there were 30. Despite this, the first-floor Flamingo beats its competitors, and not just because of location. Some 40 guests are catered for with a kitchen, fridge and cooker, laundry, a comfortable common room with TV, two free Internet terminals, and clean, modern bathrooms. They are also entertained with regular events, the fun element at the Flamingo underlined by the display of Kodak shots of visitors in party mode. Reception is 24 hours and the management also run a number of comfortable apartments in Floriańska. Here, dorm beds (max 10 to a room) start at 45zt. *Ul.Szewska 4.* ☎ *012-422-00-00. www.flamingo-hostel.com. 8 units/40 beds. Doubles 80–90zł. AE, DC, MC, V. Map p 133.*

★ Floryan OLD TOWN

What the Floryan lacks in add-ons it makes up for with location, near the Floriańska Gate a five-minute walk from the main square. Thanks to some inventive shopping at IKEA, the rooms are surprisingly comfortable, considering this is a 16th-century building—the medieval cellar now housing the Vesuvio restaurant and its wood-fire pizza oven has been used as a hostelry for centuries. The lobby is where you book for Crazy Guides's tours of Nowa Huta. *Ul.Floriańska*

Grand Hotel.

The folky Kolory, above Les Couleurs Café.

38. ☎ 012-431-14-18. *www.floryan. com.pl. 21 units. Doubles 320–470zł. AE, DC, MC, V. Map p 133.*

★★★ **Grand Hotel** Renovated in 1990, a century after its conversion from the Czartoryski Palace to the most luxurious hotel in the region, the Grand was the place to stay and be seen. Running water in the rooms, a glass-roofed restaurant and a café attracted the famous writers of the day, including Joseph Conrad. Occupied by the Nazis and left to decay afterwards, the Grand is now restored to its former glory. Its nine suites contain the furniture, stained glass, crystal, mirrors and stucco of the original Czartoryski Palace, while the rooms echo the era with ornaments and tapestries redolent of the 19th century. The lobby, the restaurant, the café, the conference and banqueting halls and the public areas attract a classy clientele and film crews—this was the first hotel in town to gain a five-star status, in 2004. Pop in for a Viennese coffee or look for cheaper rates in quieter periods. *Ul.Sławkowska 5-7.* ☎ *012-421-72-55. www.grand.pl. 62 units. Doubles 800zł. AE, DC, MC, V. Map p 133.*

★ **Greg & Tom Hostel** NEAR OLD TOWN   This award-winning hostel near the train station suits the short- and long-term visitor alike. Spacious dorm rooms, breakfast until 11am,

free tea and coffee, kitchen facilities including a fridge, cooker, microwave and toaster, laundry, two free internet terminals, Greg & Tom has come a long way since a modest house of 12 beds was opened in 2004. Now it can offer three new double rooms, with extra rooms in the Old Town to deal with the overflow. Stag parties are not welcome—otherwise, this is as hospitable and as convivial as it gets for the price. Dorm beds are 50–60zł. *Ul.Pawia 12/7.* ☎ *012-422- 41-00. www.gregtomhostel.com. 3 units/23 beds. Doubles 160zł. AE, DC, MC, V. Map p 133.*

★★★ **Gródek** OLD TOWN   A more cozy stay in the Old Town, you could not imagine. A boutique hotel in the Donimirski group, the Gródek comprises 23 rooms in a property dating back to the 11th century. Once the residency of the Tarnowski family, then part of the Dominican convent, the building feels solid and historic. The medieval clay pots, figures and tiles unearthed with the hotel conversion in 2004 are on display in the classy Cul-De-Sac restaurant downstairs, where a superior breakfast is served until mid-morning. All rooms have heated bathroom floors—most have bathtubs as well. Complimentary tea and coffee are provided in each. Units get smarter and pricier as you ascend,

The Best Lodging

until you reach a lovely roof terrace open to all. There is also a cluster of three that can be blocked off and hired as a family. *Ul.na Gródku 4.* ☎ *012-431-90-30. www.donimirski. com. 23 units. Doubles 590–890zł. AE, DC, MC, V. Map p 133.*

★ Ibis Kraków Centrum NOWY

ŚWIAT   All rooms and public areas have been renovated at this French-chain hotel, so breakfast (from 4am), a drink or a meal at the terrace L'Est-aminet is a comfortable pleasure rather than a cramped necessity. The location is great too, right by the river, within easy reach of Wawel, Kazimierz and the Old Town. All rooms have flat-screen TVs, free internet access and nice big beds, and you can call up room service for snacks 24 hours a day. For the price, you can't do better. *Ul.Syrkomil 2.* ☎ *012-299-33-00. www.ibishotel. com. 175 units. Doubles 209–299zł. AE, DC, MC, V. Map p 134.*

★★ Kolory Bed & Breakfast

KAZIMIERZ   Thirteen spacious rooms, well furnished with folky designs and artifacts, are set above Les Couleurs café, right on Plac Nowy, the heart of everything that's happening in Kazimierz. Breakfast, fresh, fluffy croissants, decent coffee

and fruit juice, is taken downstairs, where you can check emails—although there is also access—in your room. Each guest room also has its own bathroom, satellite TV and air-conditioning. If you're the sociable type, you won't find a better base in all Krakow. *Ul.Estery 10.* ☎ *012-421-04-65. www.kolory.com.pl. 13 units. Doubles 190zł. AE, DC, MC, V. Map p 133.*

★★ Maltański NEAR OLD TOWN

The Maltese was the first of the historic buildings of the boutique Donimirski group to be converted into a hotel, in 2000, and looks as classy now as it did then. The tiled floors, the original art in each room, the leafy terrace where breakfast is taken in warmer months, the Maltański offers as convivial a three-star stay as you'll find anywhere in Krakow. The usual Donimirski touches are also provided, such as free internet access, and teas and coffees in each room, plus heated bathroom floors and fluffy bath-robes. *Ul.Straszewskiego 14.* ☎ *012-431-00-10. www.donimirski.com. 16 units. Doubles 420–640zł. AE, DC, MC, V. Map p 133.*

Matejko NEAR OLD TOWN   Facili-ties, furnishings and services have all

Hotel Monopol.

The converted 19th-century Ostoya Palace Hotel.

been significantly improved at this pretty townhouse just outside the Old Town. Laundry, baby-sitting, sauna and massage can now all be provided, while guest rooms are bright and comfortably furnished. A bar, beer garden and restaurant make for one of the nicest and most convenient three-star stays in town. *Pl.Matejki 8.* ☎ *012-422-47-37. www. matejkohotel.pl. 48 units. Doubles 320–420zł. AE, DC, MC, V. Map p 133.*

Monopol NEAR OLD TOWN If anything indicates Krakow's transformation this past decade, it is the conversion of this once shabby, state-owned eyesore to a pretty, comfortable, mid-range, city-center lodging the match of any in town in the same price bracket. A standard range of services (laundry, tour booking, parking) is provided with a smile by a friendly staff—another pleasant change from the bad old days. *Ul.Św Gertrudy 6.* ☎ *012-422-76-66. www.rthotels.com.pl. 75 units. Doubles 260–355zł. AE, DC, MC, V. Map p 133.*

★ **Nathan's Villa Hostel** STRADOM Between the southern fringe of the city center and the northern edge of Kazimierz, this is one of Krakow's most attractive hostels, offering an impressive array of free services. Complimentary laundry is a huge boon for the passing backpacker, but those staying a little longer can take advantage of the ping-pong and pool tables, a movie lounge, varied events nights, WiFi and the fully-fitted kitchen. The clean bathrooms are equipped with powerful showers, better than in most three-star hotels. Dorm beds range from 50zł to 60zł depending on the time of year. *Ul.Św.Agnieszki 1.* ☎ *012-422-35-45. www.nathans villa.com. 21 units/118 dorm beds. Doubles 180zł. AE, DC, MC, V. Map p 133.*

★ **Novotel Centrum** NOWY ŚWIAT Near its French-chain sister the Ibis Centrum, this well-facilitated riverside hotel suits business traveler and family alike. A pool, Jacuzzi, gym, sauna and playroom all open from early in the day, and video games are available in each of the 98 bright and neatly furnished rooms. Brasserie and bar are equally bright and light-filled, while some rooms on the upper floors have great views of Wawel Castle just the other side of a bend in the river. *Ul.Kościuszki 5.* ☎ *012-299-29-00. www.orbisonline.pl. 198 units. Doubles 340–700zł. AE, DC, MC, V. Map p 134.*

★ **Ostoya Palace Hotel** NEAR OLD TOWN Another hotel conversion of a 19th-century palace, but all the same a welcome addition to accommodation options in the luxury bracket. Architect Józef Pokutyński's opulent Ostaszewski Palace was completed in 1895, but sadly allowed to lapse into decay after the Second World War. Its recent renovation has seen it transformed into 24 four-star rooms in soothing pastel colors, all with heated bathroom floors, some with separate tubs and showers. A sauna is also provided, while the bar, restaurant and patio are done out in similar historic style. *Ul.Piłsudskiego 24.* ☎ *012-430-90-00. www.ostoya palace.pl. 24 units. Doubles 640–775zł. AE, DC, MC, V. Map p 134.*

★★★ Pałac Bonerowski. OLD

TOWN On the corner of the market square and Św.Jana, this historic three-story, five-star comprises eight standard rooms and six large suites, most featuring architectural detail installed as the property passed through various well-to-do families over the centuries. Celebrations for the victory over the Turks at Vienna in 1683 were prepared here. The most recent renovation came when the palace was converted into a hotel in 2005, the grand staircase and chandeliers back in regular use. Contemporary additions—Finnish and steam saunas, plasma TVs, broadband internet—complement an unsurpassed view of the square. *Ul.Św.Jana 1.* ☎ *012-374-13-00. www.palacbonerowski.pl. 14 units. Doubles 730–830zł. AE, DC, MC, V. Map p 133.*

★★ Pod Róza OLD TOWN Tsar

Alexander I, Franz Liszt and Honoré de Balzac have all passed through this grand doorway on Floriańska— the Pod Róza is one of three vintage properties delicately renovated and converted (with a lift) by the Likus

group. Ornaments and textiles embellish the sense of grandeur and history, an atmosphere that extends to the first-class restaurant set over two floors in the lobby atrium, the café and the wine cellar. *Ul.Floriańska 14.* ☎ *012-424-33-00. www.hotel. com.pl. 64 units. Doubles 720zł–850zł. AE, DC, MC, V. Map p 133.*

★ Pod Wawelem NEAR WAWEL

Regularly featured as a cheap option on generic hotel booking sites, 'Beneath Wawel' is a good find. Within a short walk of Wawel, the Old Town and a pleasant river- side stroll from Kazimierz, this com- fortable three-star offers waterfront views from many of its 48 tidy rooms. Guests are entitled to a mod- est discount at the contemporary Lemonday restaurant, whose stan- dard would more befit a four-star. Further amenities include a modest basement gym and sauna. *Pl.Na Groblach 22.* ☎ *012-426-26-25. www.hotelpodwawelem.pl. 48 units. Doubles 310–520zł. AE, DC, MC, V. Map p 134.*

★ Poleski DĘBNIKI Opened in

late 2006, this is one of the few hotels in Krakow to make great use of a riverside location. Immediately opposite Wawel (rooms without a castle view are about 50zł cheaper), the three-star Poleski has little- known restaurant whose continuous

Stained-glass Wyspiański windows at Pollera.

PTTK Wyspiański, near Old Town.

window seems to run the entire length of the Vistula. The rooms are on the comfortable side of functional, with standard fittings, but any sense of claustrophobia is alleviated by the fourth-floor panoramic terrace. *Ul.Sandormierska 6.* ☎ *012-260-54-05. www.hotelpoleski.pl. 20 units. Doubles 309–519zł. AE, DC, MC, V. Map p 134.*

★ **Pollera** OLD TOWN When Kasper Pollera first opened this hotel, Napoleon had not long been buried. Enjoying its grand period a century ago before being occupied by the Nazis, then left to decay, the hardy Pollera has been handed back to its rightful owners and brought back into service. Guests are treated to comfortable if not luxurious lodgings, but most are happy to pass by the wonderful original stained-glass artwork by Stanisław Wyspiański on the staircase while contemplating 180 years of history. *Ul.Szpitalna 30.* ☎ *012-422-10-44. www.pollera.com. pl. 42 units. Doubles 360–450zł. AE, DC, MC, V. Map p 133.*

Polonia NEAR OLD TOWN Opened opposite the train station in 1917, the Polonia is one of several hotels in town gradually shedding decades of post-war neglect. The rooms are mixed bag of modernized and vintage, though none are tatty and the location on the edge of the Old

Town can't be beat. *Ul.Basztowa 25.* ☎ *012-422-12-33. www.hotel-polonia.com.pl. 62 units. Doubles 260–324zł. AE, DC, MC, V. Map p 133.*

PTTK Wyspiański NEAR OLD TOWN Built in the 1960s, this behemoth on the Planty ring was completely renovated in 2003 and now operates as an attractive three-star conference hotel. Coachloads of tourists pull up in the wide forecourt all year round—individual travelers should look out for online deals and all-in packages set around special events in town. *Ul.Westerplatte 15.* ☎ *012-422-95-66. www. hotel-wyspianski.pl. 158 units. Doubles 195–440zł. AE, DC, MC, V. Map p 133.*

★★★ **Pugetów** NEAR OLD TOWN The jewel in the Donimirski crown, the outstanding Pugetów was opened in 2003, in one of a cluster of 19th-century buildings set in from the main road linking the Old Town to Kazimierz. Each of its seven rooms has been individually furnished in historic style according to character name—Napoleon's Polish lover Pani Walewska or Joseph Conrad, for example. The result encourages repeat custom all year round. This is honeymoon material, so relax and enjoy one of the most impressive lodgings in all Poland. *Ul.Starowiślna*

15a. ☎ 012-432-49-50. www. donimirski.com. 7 units. Doubles 410–510zł. AE, DC, MC, V. Map p 133.

★★★ **Qubus Hotel** PODGÓRZE Best spa and pool in the city, if only for the rooftop panorama as you swim your lengths, laze in the Jacuzzi or stretch out on the recliners. Below this seventh-floor treat, the Qubus goes about things in a suitably business-like fashion, serving a first-class breakfast in the Ogień restaurant, decent cocktails in the Barracuda lobby bar, and providing entertainment in the Mile Stone jazz club and After Work bar. Snag a bargain if you book in advance online or from a generic hotel-booking website. Ul.Nadwiślańska 6. ☎ 012-374-51-00. www.qubushotel.com. 194 units. Doubles 490zł. AE, DC, MC, V. Map p 134.

★ **Radisson SAS** NEAR OLD TOWN You know what you're getting with a Radisson, this new one stood prominently on the edge of the Planty ring just outside the Old Town. Along with the expected quality of service and fare in the Milk&Co and Salt&Co bar and restaurant, Individuality has been added with local artwork in each of the 196 rooms. Ul.Straszewkiego 17. ☎ 012-618-88-88. www.radissonsas.com. 196 units. Doubles 480–880zł. AE, DC, MC, V. Map p 133.

Regent KAZIMIERZ Handily located near the action in Kazimierz, the Regent is the one in the RT chain most in need of renovation—bathroom and electrical fittings in some rooms could do with an overhaul, as could the furnishings. For all that, the desk staff are wonderfully friendly and online bargains mean that you've got a base where you most need it for half of what it would cost to stay on Szeroka. Ul.Bożego Ciała 1. ☎ 012-430-62-34. www.rt hotels.pl. 39 units. Doubles 222–330zł. AE, DC, MC, V. Map p 133.

Rezydent OLD TOWN Close to the main market square, this standard RT chain hotel is most conveniently situated, its rooms having enjoyed a recent and welcome renovation. Little wrong with the restaurant, the Pod Gwiazdami, where hotel guests

Radisson SAS.

receive a handy discount. *Ul.Grodzka 9.* ☎ *012-429-54-10. www.polhotels. com/Cracow/Rezydent. 59 units. Doubles 287–388zł. AE, DC, MC, V. Map p 133.*

★★ **Rubinstein** KAZIMIERZ Italian marble in the bathrooms, carpets of New Zealand wool in the bedrooms, and neo-Renaissance touches throughout, this is the most stylish place to stay in Kazimierz. Room rates reflect the high standard but in the quieter summer weeks you should be able to find a bargain online. No beating the location either, the whole of the Jewish quarter spread out before you from the roof terrace. The quality bar and restaurant complete the picture. *Ul.Szeroka 12.* ☎ *012-384-00-00. www.hotelrubinstein.com. 29 units. Doubles 460–700zł. AE, DC, MC, V. Map p 133.*

★★ **Senacki** OLD TOWN A conversion of a historic building on the Royal Route, the Senacki comprises 20 finely decorated rooms, including two luxury ones, a penthouse and the cheaper attic. The lack of a lift keeps the Senacki at three-star status—but the frequently returning visitors know class when they see it. The restaurant receives healthy custom from non-residents. *Ul.Grodzka 51.* ☎ *012-422-76-86. www.senacki. krakow.pl. 20 units. Doubles 280–520zł. AE, DC, MC, V. Map p 133.*

★★ **Sheraton Kraków** NEAR WAWEL Set by the Vistula just under Wawel, the Sheraton accommodates guests to its usual high standards. High-speed internet in 232 comfortable rooms, separate saunas for men and women, a heated indoor pool and a range of massage treatments are key here, while non-residents are brought in by the 200 odd vodkas available the QUBE bar, the Tex-Mex food and TV sports at the SomePlace Else bar,

The Stary is a converted 15th century merchant's house.

and the Med cuisine on offer at The Olive. *Ul.Powiśle 7.* ☎ *012-662-10-00. www.sheraton.com/krakow. 232 units. Doubles 440–915zł. AE, DC, MC, V. Map p 134.*

★★★ **Stary** OLD TOWN Quite possibly the best hotel in Krakow, if not in Poland itself, the Stary is a converted merchant's house, originally built in the 15th century. The Likus group has really gone to town—a glass lift, marble, silk, exotic woods and Oriental carpets, two heated pools (one with massage jets), a salt cave, Finnish and steam saunas and yoga among the many treatments. Even the single rooms have Jacuzzi tubs. In summer they open a rooftop terrace with bar—in colder months, the quality Trzy Rybki restaurant more than compensates. *Ul.Szczepańska 5.* ☎ *012-384-08-08. www.stary-hotel. com.pl. 53 units. Doubles 765–815zł. AE, DC, MC, V. Map p 133.*

★ **Tango House** OLD TOWN So close to the main market square you can hear the bugler, this is one of the city's best bed and breakfasts. Converted in 2007 from a 16th-century property—Krakow's first

The 16th-century Tango House, originally Krakow's first bath-house.

public bathhouse, in fact—the Tango House is decked out in bright colors and contemporary furnishings. Ambient tango music can be switched on with the push of a dial. A decent cold buffet is laid out for breakfast and a laptop is provided for guests' use in the café. *Ul.Szpi-talna 4. ☎ 012-429-31-14. www. tangohouse.pl. 8 units. Doubles 260–380zł. AE, DC, MC, V. Map p 133.*

★ **Trecius** OLD TOWN Named after the secretary to István Batory acknowledged to have lived here in the 16th century, this townhouse was probably built 300 years earlier. Set on the corner of Floriańska and Św.Tomasza, it's one of Krakow's best located and most characterful guesthouses—you can even make out some of the 13th-century brick-work amid the exposed stones. All eight rooms have been kitted out with contemporary touches—satel-lite TV, internet and heated bath-room floors—and a flick through the visitors' book should assure you of the hotel's conviviality.

Ul.Św.Tomasza 18. ☎ 012-421-25-21. www.trecius.krakow.pl. 8 units. Doubles 200–300zł. AE, DC, MC, V. Map p 133.

★ **Wawel** OLD TOWN In private hands for more than a decade, this former 19th-century inn has under-gone many improvements and today ranks as one of the best mid-range deals in Krakow. Guest rooms are spa-cious and homely, in calming colors and equipped with flat-screen TVs. The Jacuzzi and steam rooms are paid extras. *Ul.Poselska 22. ☎ 012-424-13-00. www.hotelwawel.pl. 39 units. Doubles 370–520zł. AE, DC, MC, V. Map p 133.*

★★★ **Wentzl** OLD TOWN Right-fully considered one of the finest lodgings in all Poland, this sumptuous 200-year-old landmark comprises 18 opulent guest rooms, many overlook-ing the main square. Dark woods, richly colored rugs and parquet floors feature throughout. Staff are used to dealing with dignitaries and impor-tant guests, and will happily book your theatre ticket or city tour. The in-house terrace restaurant is a destina-tion in itself. *Rynek Główny 19. ☎ 012-430-26-64. www.wentzl.pl. 18 units. Doubles 535–615zł. AE, DC, MC, V. Map p 133.* ●

The sumptuous Wentzl.

10 The Best Day Trips & Excursions

Auschwitz

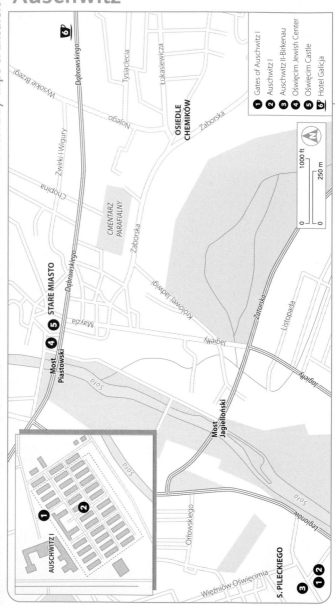

1 Gates of Auschwitz I
2 Auschwitz I
3 Auschwitz II-Birkenau
4 Oświęcim Jewish Center
5 Oświęcim Castle
6 Hotel Galicja

OSIEDLE CHEMIKÓW

CMENTARZ PARAFIALNY

STARE MIASTO

Most Piastowski

Most Jagielloński

AUSCHWITZ I

S. PILECKIEGO

Wysokie Brzegi
Dąbrowskiego
Tysiąclecia
Łukasiewicza
Zaborska
Nojgo
Zwirki i Wigury
Chopina
Dąbrowskiego
Zaborska
Królowej Jadwigi
Zatorska
Listopada
Mayzla
Jagiełły
Jagiełły
Soła
Soła
Soła
Soła
Legionów
Orłowskiego
Wieźniów Oświęcimia

0   250 m
0   1000 ft

Preserved as a museum in 1947 as it was found—'Arbeit Macht Frei' gate and all—Auschwitz attracts busloads of tourists, many on all-in tours from nearby Krakow. For independent visits, a guide is essential, but not obligatory. Two camps sit 3km apart: Auschwitz I, its huts and one surviving gas chamber; and vast Auschwitz II-Birkenau, whose guard tower, gate and rails remain. Auschwitz (Oświęcim) is a town in its own right, a 'City of Peace' with two key sites: the Jewish Center and a modest castle.

❶ ★★ Gates of Auschwitz I— 'Arbeit Macht Frei'. Nearly everyone standing at these gates has seen these gates in film or photo form—to stand here, before the hour-long tour of the first and best preserved camp, is a chilling feeling. The motto, 'Work Makes You Free', was used at other camps. Here, bizarrely, it is used in a 1920s' typeface with an upside-down 'B' in 'Arbeit'. Just inside the gates are drawings by Mieczław Kościelniak (1912–1993), Auschwitz survivor, founder of the museum and an artist of global renown. An orchestra would play at the beginning of the working day—and at the end, inmates carrying the corpses of their exhausted colleagues. ⏱ *10 min.*

❷ ★★★ Auschwitz I. Concentration camps in the Nazi Reich were used for either slave labor or immediate execution. Auschwitz was both a work camp and a death camp. It comprises neat rows of 28 huts, half converted for public display, either by theme ('Everyday Life of the Prisoner', 'Extermination') or provenance (Poland, Yugoslavia, European Roma). Tours also take in Death Block 11; Assembly Square with a reconstruction of its portable gallows; and the one remaining gas chamber of the original four. You may have to wait outside one block as tour groups file out. Of particular resonance are the suitcases, piles of human hair and children's shoes, as

found by Soviet soldiers in 1945; the starvation cells of block 11, in particular number 18 where Polish priest Maximilian Kolbe sacrificed his life for a fellow prisoner; and the adjoining Wall of Death, against which thousands of prisoners were shot, today strewn with flowers and flags in the colors of the Auschwitz prisoners' uniforms, blue and white. Nothing, though, can match the feeling of walking into the bare gas chamber, cramped, claustrophobic, a track on its floor leading a few meters to the ovens alongside. This is the last stop on any tour. There is a café and souvenir shop by the museum entrance, and more amenities across the car park. ⏱ *1 hr. Ul.Więźniów Oświęcim 20 ☎ 033-844-80-00. www.auschwitz.org.pl. Admission free; individual guided tours 39zł; groups vary. Daily June–Aug 8am–7pm; May, Sept 8am–6pm; Apr, Oct 8am–5pm; Mar, Nov 8am–4pm; Dec–Feb 8am–3pm. Children under 12 advised not to enter. All buses, trains and minibuses to Oświęcim. Frequent guided tours from Krakow.*

❸ ★★★ Auschwitz II-Birkenau. Birkenau was built to cope with the huge influx of European Jewry, particularly from Hungary. It was little but a death factory—you can see the rails leading from the gates to the crematorium. Climb the stairs to the watchtower over the gates and there are brick stumps as

Practical Matters: Auschwitz

Auschwitz, Polish name on maps, signs and timetables Oświęcim, is 75 kilometers from Krakow. Nearly all tour companies offer guided visits to Auschwitz, for about 90zł. Allow half a day. Regular city buses leave from ul.Bosacka behind the train station, for Oświęcim train and bus stations, 90 minutes journey time. Some call at Auschwitz I. A less frequent train service takes the same time and costs around the same, less than 15zł. A dozen local buses link Oświęcim station with Auschwitz I. Oświęcim town center is on the east bank of the river from the train station. Those on guided tours from Krakow are bussed the 3km from Auschwitz I-Birkenau; for independent visitors, an hourly shuttle bus runs from mid-April to November. A taxi should cost 15zł.

far as the eye can see, remnants of the barracks that held prisoners in conditions barely fit for cattle. Your guide will point out the gaps between roof and thin wall of the example hut—there was little difference between the temperature outside and in. At full capacity, the ovens consumed 60,000 victims a day. On the camp's northern fringe is a pond still gray from the human ashes dumped there. Birkenau is bare, lacking in tourist amenities but worth a visit if only to appreciate the scale of what transpired. ⏱ *40 min. Same details as above.*

❹ ★★ Oświęcim Jewish Center. Opened in 2000, the year that the last Jewish resident of **Oświęcim, Szymon Kluger (1925–2000),** died, and set beside the town's only surviving synagogue, this laudable institution is

Auschwitz II-Birkenau's rails and guard tower.

Panel of photographs in the Sauna, at the former Nazi concentration camp, Auschwitz-Birkenau.

dedicated to keeping local Jewish culture alive. A video of interviews with surviving residents is shown in English, the main attraction of the museum also filled with photographs, documents and sundry artifacts relating to pre-war life in Oświęcim, whose local population of 15,000 in 1939 was half Jewish. Soon after, the Nazis converted the Synagogue into a munitions warehouse, and the Communists into a carpet warehouse—it was returned to the Jewish community and restored for 2000. Although services are no longer given, this is considered a place of sanctuary. A nearby Education Center hosts seminars, talks and cultural events. Opposite the museum, you can visit Kluger's house as he left it in 2000. ⏱ *45 min. Pl.ks.Jana Skarbka 3-5* ☎ *033-844-70-02. www.ajcf.pl. Train or bus to Oświęcim.*

⑤ ★ Oświęcim Castle. Set between the Jewish Center and Synagogue and the Sola river it overlooks, Oświęcim Castle demonstrates the generations of citizens who lived here. Its 13th-century Gothic tower, currently being renovated, was built after the Tartar invasion, and other elements were added after further invasion, fire and flood: defensive walls, a moat, armory and living quarters. A modest historical exhibition awaits expansion once current renovations are complete. Tours from Krakow do not go into Oświęcim town—you are generally welcome to ask the guide to drop you off at the station—a short walk over the river from town—and make your own way back. ⏱ *30 min. Ul.Zamkowa 1* ☎ *033-842-44-27. Train or bus to Oświęcim.*

⑥ ★ Hotel Galicja. The best hotel in town, a renovated old post house, provides the best spots to eat and drink in Oseswiercim town: the U Szwejka cellar pub with original 19th-century brick walls; and the first-floor Stara Poczta restaurant, serving traditional Polish and Silesian favorites. It's far nearer the bus station than the train, so if you're returning to Krakow under your own steam, and ending your visit here (there are 32 rooms too), bus is the best way back. *Ul.Dąbrowskiego 119, Oświęcim.* ☎ *030-843-61-15. www.hotelgalicja.com. $$.*

Ojców

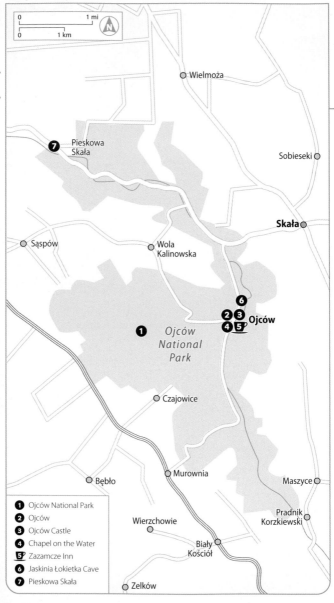

1. Ojców National Park
2. Ojców
3. Ojców Castle
4. Chapel on the Water
5. Zazamcze Inn
6. Jaskinia Łokietka Cave
7. Pieskowa Skała

Ojców, Krakow's closest national park, is associated with rocks and royals. Some 21 km² of limestone and woodland in the river valley of the Prądnik, its caves hid King Władisłw Łokietek from the Bohemians. Naming the area after 'father of the rocks', his son, Kazimierz the Great, set about building a series of 25 castles, today called the Eagle Nests Trail, a leading attraction. Many visitors also travel the 35km from Krakow for the wildlife, the bats and the birds, the beetles and the butterflies, that call the hundreds of caves and unspoiled hills home.

❶ ★★★ Ojców National Park. Poland's smallest national park, a short and easy hop north from Krakow, comprises the limestone valley of the Prądnik river, the hundreds of caves and weird rock formations it has created and the abundance of wildlife and plant varieties engendered by its microclimate. It is also the southern fringe of the Eagle Nests Trail, a 165-km long string of 25 medieval strongholds commissioned by Kazimir the Great, now a popular route for hikers and cyclists. A ruined one stands outside the village of Ojców, administrative base for the surrounding park. One of the most stunning is

Pieskowa Skała, built in Renaissance style at the northern border of the national park. ⏱ *2 hr. 32-047 Ojców.* ☎ *012-389-20-05. www.ojcow.pl. Admission free. Guided day tours in English 450zł. Bus or train from Krakow to Ojców.*

❷ ★★ Ojców. Set in the centre of the park, the pretty village of Ojców sits in the Prądnik Valley, a community of 220 souls living in wooden chalets set against a fabulous backdrop of woods and cliffs. It's a treat in autumn or winter—and filled with hikers, bikers and parties of schoolchildren all year round. For all its natural beauty, this modest settlement

Ojców National Park.

Practical Matters: Ojców

Ojców village is 35 km north of Krakow. Two buses a day leave from Krakow bus station, behind the train station, for Olkusz, calling at Ojców after an hour. Eight buses a day go to Ojców Park, two fast ones early in the morning taking 40 mins. By car (40 mins), head north past IKEA and Macro until you hit the roundabout turn for Olkusz, keeping on road 94. Ojców is soon signposted. Bicycles can follow this same route, but a nicer one is along the Eagle Nests Trail, heading from Krowodrza along side roads—you'll find a map on *www.ojcow.pl*. There's also a fast bike route via road 794—again, check the website.

has a surprising number of man-made attractions. By the bus terminus, Władysław Szafer's natural history museum (closed Mon, also Sat, Sun in winter) contains remains of mammoths and other prehistoric creatures; nearby are the tourist office and a regional museum lined with folk costumes and old prints of the village. The main draws are ruined Ojców Castle and the nearby Chapel on the Water, attracting thousands to Ojców every summer.

Gate house, Ojców Castle.

🕐 *1 hr. Tourist office Ojców 15.*
📞 *012-389-20-10. www.ojcow.pttk.pl. Bus or train from Krakow to Ojców.*

3 ★ **Ojców Castle.** The southernmost of the string of strongholds built by Kazimir the Great, Ojców is a Gothic ruin, its original towers still erect and ringed by bats. Also standing are the gatehouse and walls of the keep—the moat and well have since been filled in. Although most of the walls collapsed in the 1820s, the castle is still worth a visit for the gloomy, historic atmosphere and the view of the woods and the valley.
🕐 *30 min.* 📞 *012-389-20-05. Admission 2.50zł/1.50zł. Tue-Sun Apr–May, Aug–Sept 10am–4.45pm, June–July 10am–5.45pm, Oct 10am–3.45pm.*

4 ★★ **Chapel on the Water.** This anomaly was opened in 1901, a rustic chapel perched over the Prądnik river as the then ruling Tsar Nikolai II had forbidden the building of any places of worship in regional territory–on land at least. The building is in the shape of a cross, conforming to so-called Ojców style. You can take a peek at the interior in between services on Sundays. 🕐 *20 min.*

5 ★ **Zazamcze Inn.** Easily the best dining option around these parts is this pretty chalet surrounded by greenery, known for its grilled trout and barbecued pork. This is quality fare in a quality setting—hence the wedding parties and tourist groups. There are a dozen rooms too, should you choose to stay over. You'll find it just outside Ojców. *Ojców 1b.* ☎ *012-389-20-83. $.*

6 ★ **Jaskinia Łokietka Cave.** Some 2.5 km from Ojców village, a 45-minute walk, this is the largest and most famous of the hundreds of caves dotted around the national park. Named after the so-called King 'Shorty' (Łokietek), Kazimir's father who allegedly hid here from Bohemian Vaclav II, this illuminated cave is some 250 m long. Visits are guided only and last about 30 minutes—take warm clothes as the temperature is a less than 10 °C. There are said to be seven breeds of bats resident here for centuries. ⏱ *20 min* ☎ *012-419-08-01. Admission 7zł/5zł. Daily spring,*

autumn 9am–3.30pm/4.30pm, summer 9am–6.30pm.

7 ★★★ **Pieskowa Skała.** The jewel in Ojców's crown, and a rare perfectly preserved castle in the Eagle Nests Trail, stands 9 km from Ojców village, an easy 45-minute walk away. On your way you'll pass the limestone pillar known as Hercules' Club—the castle is just behind. Once a stronghold in the medieval fashion, under the aristocratic Szafraniec family, it gained an arcaded Renaissance courtyard. Equally attractive to the thousands of annual tourists is the exhibition of European art contained here, part of the Wawel collection, featuring Baroque rooms lined with fine Flemish tapestries showing the life of Alexander the Great, and Gothic carvings from the 1400s. A second floor will cover the period from the 18th century to the early 20th once it is completed. A stroll around the fine gardens should round off your visit nicely. ⏱ *40 min. Ul.Sułoszowa 4.* ☎ *012-389-60-04. Admission 10zł/7zł. Tue–Fri 10am–3.30pm. Summer also Sat–Sun 10am–5.30pm.*

Pieskowa Skała.

Zakopane

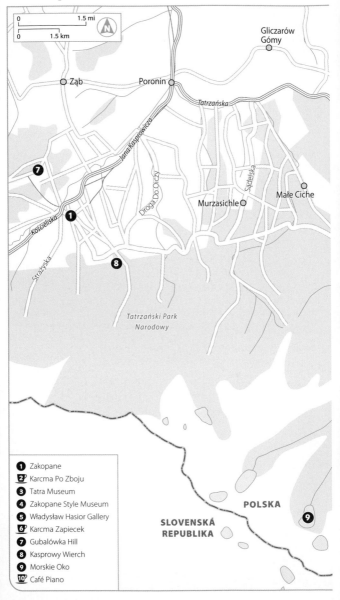

0 ____ 1.5 mi
0 ____ 1.5 km

Gliczarów
Gómy

Ząb   Poronin

Tatrzańska

Jana Kasprowicza

Droga Do Olczy

Sądelska

Murzasichle

Małe Ciche

Kościeliska

Strążyska

Tatrzański Park
Narodowy

POLSKA

SLOVENSKÁ
REPUBLIKA

1 Zakopane
2 Karcma Po Zboju
3 Tatra Museum
4 Zakopane Style Museum
5 Władysław Hasior Gallery
6 Karcma Zapiecek
7 Gubalówka Hill
8 Kasprowy Wierch
9 Morskie Oko
10 Café Piano

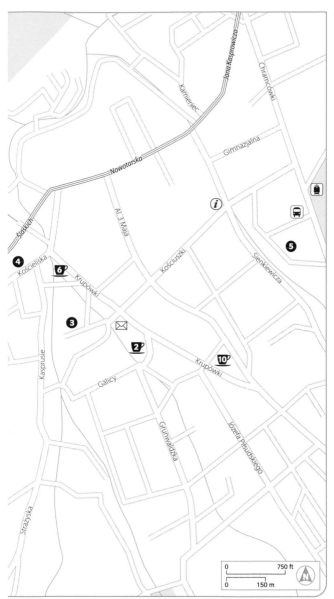

The highest town in Poland, down south by the Slovak border, Zakopane is where Poles go to ski, hike and hang out for the weekend—often, it feels, at the very same weekend. Expect queues and traffic jams on major winter breaks. The gateway to the Tatra mountains, the only Alpine range in the region, Zakopane allows easy access for the funicular to the Gubalówka Hill. A longer stroll or short hop on the bus bring you to the cable car from Kużnice and the summit of Kasprowy Wierch, then the glacial lake of Morskie Oko.

❶ ★★★ kids Zakopane. With regular buses and trains a 3 hr journey from Krakow, and roads jam-packed for winter weekends, Zakopane is southern Poland's favorite getaway. Its skiing facilities so plentiful it was a reasonable candidate for a recent Winter Olympics, Zakopane has a century of experience in accommodating tourists. First the fresh air began attracting hikers and health tourists here on doctor's advice in the 1870s; then a bohemian atmosphere arose when writers and artists from the Młoda Polska movement used Zakopane as a place to create, make merry and foment revolution. Today the town center, and its main street of Krupówki, still display both the chalet charm of those days and the commercial clout of a major tourist destination. Within walking distance of the bus and train stations to the east of the Krupówki hub are a handful of worthwhile regional museums and galleries, and a funicular to Gubalówka Hill, the closest and busiest summit. A 20 min walk south of town, regularly served by local buses, is the small village of Kużnice, site of the busy cable car to Kasprowy Wierch, the highest of the near 2,000m peaks forming the border with Slovakia. *Tourist information ul.Kościuszki 17.* ☎ *018-201-22-11. www.zakopane.pl. All buses and trains to Zakopane.*

❷ ★ kids Karcma Po Zboju. On the main drag, this bar-restaurant in traditional style offers local specialties from breakfast (white sausage,

Traditional house in Zakopane.

Trekking in the Tatra mountains.

the famed local cheeses) onwards. Cakes, pies and puddings are another strong point. A garden in equally rustic style contains a see-saw, slide and little treehouse. An ideal first port of call to freshen up after your arrival, get your bearings and get acquainted with the locality. *Ul.Krupówki 22b.* ☎ *012-201-61-40. $$.*

❸ ★★ **Tatra Museum.** The distinguished Tatra Museum is formed of several divisions, including the Zakopane Style Museum and Hasior Gallery, with information for each found on the same website. This main branch is of historical interest in itself—the building was designed by Stanisław Witkiewicz (1885–1939), an influential painter, playwright and architect of the pre-war Zakopane circle. Inside, two floors display the history of the region through the ages, from prehistoric traces to Zakopane's heyday in the late 1800s. The rapid rise of tourism and culture are covered hand-in-hand—the development of sanatoria and skiing, as well as a theater company and a local press. A replica of a typical cottage, plus examples of ceramics, tools and traditional costumes, show the way of life that attracted so many here from Krakow in the early 20th century—Zakopane was where Poles could express their patriotism openly. The top floor deals with

Practical Matters: Zakopane

Zakopane town is served by buses every hour from Krakow, regular journey time around 2.5 hrs, tickets about 15zł. Traffic jams on busy winter weekends are frequent—allow 3 hrs. The drive via roads 7 and 47 should be 90 mins. If you're thinking of hiring a car, Zakopane has a decent supply of parking places but the town itself is easily walkable and bus services are cheap and regular to nearby attractions. Private rooms, pensions, hostels and hotels are equally plentiful but it pays to book ahead in high season, summer or winter.

natural history, showing the geology of the mountain range, examples of local plants and stuffed animals, the protected Tatra chamois goat and so on. All in all, the museum provides a detailed and entertaining stroll through local history. ⏲ *1 hr. Ul.Krupówki 10.* ☎ *018-201-52-05. www.tatrzanskie.com.pl. Admission 7zł/5zł. July–Aug Tue, Thur, Sat 9am–5pm, Wed, Fri 9am–6pm, Sun 9am–3pm. May, June, Sept Tue–Sat 9am–5pm, Sun 9am-3pm. Oct–Apr Wed–Sat 9am–5pm, Sun 9am–3pm.*

④ ★★ Zakopane Style Museum.

Another Witkiewicz building, the Koliba Willa is an apt setting for an illustration of the architectural vernacular of Zakopane, a modern revision of traditional methods instigated by Witkiewicz himself at the turn of the past century. Many pieces were collated by estate owner Zygmunt Gnatowski, a friend of Witkiewicz, and bequeathed to the artist. The house itself went through several changes, including occupation by the Nazis, before this collection of ethnic fittings and furniture was set out by contemporary installation artist

Władysław Hasior (1928–1999) and opened as a museum in the early 1990s. It comprises two floors of seven rooms, filled with ornate but sturdy chairs and cupboards, tools and folksy tiles, curtains and light fittings. ⏲ *30 min. Koliba Willa, Ul.Kościeliska 18.* ☎ *018-201-36-02. Admission 7zł/5.50zł. Sept–June Wed–Sat 9am–5pm, Sun 9am–3pm. July–Aug Wed, Fri–Sat 9am–5pm, Thurs 9am–6pm, Sun 9am–3pm.*

⑤ ★★ Władysław Hasior Gallery.

The most well-known Zakopane artist of the 20th century, Władysław Hasior displayed many regional influences in his paintings and installations, exhibited across Europe in the 1960s and 1970s. Banners, sculptures and paintings exude bright colors and essentially Polish themes, albeit with a great deal of wit and irreverence—this was art with little censorship, as ever was in Zakopane. The gallery was opened in the mid 1980s, a decade before the artist's death. ⏲ *30 min. Ul.Koziniec 8.* ☎ *018-206-68-71. Admission 7zł/5.50zł Wed–Sat 11am–6pm, Sun 9am–3pm.*

Kasprowy Ski Resort.

Mount Kasprowy Wierch.

you can walk back down—a great deal easier than the calf-crunching, hour-long climb uphill. ⏱ *2 hr. Funicular return 20zł. Daily July–Aug 7am–9pm. Sept–June 8am–5pm.*

8 ★★★ **Kasprowy Wierch.** For the real Tatra experience, jump on one of the many buses covering the 3km journey from Zakopane to Kuźnice to ride the cable car to the 2,000 m summit of Kasprowy Wierch. The mountain forms the Polish-Slovak border—you can walk over into another country. Because of the queues in high season, many choose to walk up or down the mountain, a trek of 2–3 hours. At the top you'll find scientific observatories, opened around the same time as the cable car was installed in the 1930s, and a panoramic restaurant. A return ticket on the cable car allows you two hours at the top. A number of firms offer skiing lessons from intermediate up, and advance tickets on the cable car. See www.discover zakopane.com for details. ⏱ *2 hr.*

Morskie Oko.

6 ★ **Karcma Zapiecek.** This rustic restaurant on the main street is the ideal spot for a lunchtime stop-off to load up on carbohydrates and regional dishes made with local sheep's milk cheeses before you attack the slopes. If you're heading here in the evening for an après-ski fill-up, you might be entertained with a little live folk music. *Ul.Krupówki 43.* ☎ *012-201-56-99. $$.*

7 ★★★ **kids Gubalówka Hill.** This nursery ski run is the perfect introduction to the Tatra slopes, easily accessed by funicular a short walk from downtown Zakopane— simply stroll to the far western end of Krupówki and join the queue. At the top you'll find the terrace restaurant Gubalówka, stores selling sundry souvenirs and far too many hamburger stands for comfort. You can't beat the views of the surrounding slopes, though, and kids will enjoy the pony rides, mini bobsleigh and pay telescopes. Several hiking trails also start from here, or

Cable car return 40zł. Daily July–Aug 7.30am–8pm. Sept–June 8am–5pm.

❾ ★★★ Morskie Oko. This gorgeous glacial lake is one of Zakopane's big draws—many a restaurant in Poland serving regional highlander cuisine is named after it. The starting point for the 2 hr hike to reach it starts at a large car park at Polana Palenica (also called Polana Białczanska), connected by regular bus or minibus from Zakopane or nearby Łysa Polana. There a gaggle of hikers of all types and ages gather, before paying a couple of euros to enter the national park and the tarmac trail leading up through the trees. Local highlanders still work horse-drawn sleighs and carriages according to season from here to 1.5 km before the summit for those not keen on the walk—price negotiable. Surrounded by towering peaks, the 'Eye of the Sea' makes any climb worthwhile—it's a stunning sight. The Schronisko przy Morskim Oku mountain hut stands at the northern edge, offering bunk beds for climbers and basic domestic meals. It takes about an hour to walk around the lake and 90 mins to walk back downhill. ⏱ *4 hr.*

❿ ★ Café Piano. Pull up a velvet-seated swing at the bar counter and help yourself to a well earned beer or cocktail at the trendiest bar in Zakopane, in a little alley just off the main street. The Piano manages to combine rustic and contemporary—note the amber and touches of greenery. It's a little cramped so can get packed on busy winter weekends but that's a minor gripe. Good place too for picking up flyers and brochures for what's on in town. *Ul.Krupówki 63.* ☎ *030-252-11-55. $.* ●

Hard Cheese

Wherever you go in Zakopane, you're bound to see an old lady selling little bundles of oscypek—local cheese made from heavily salted unpasteurized sheep's milk. Each takes at least two weeks to produce, the bundle shaped into a pretty pattern, soaked in a barrel full of brine and then placed for ten days or more under the roof of a typical wooden house to be smoked slowly and thus gain its distinctive flavour. This is how oscypek has been made in the Tatras for generations. Shortly before Poland joined the EU in 2004, there was an outcry that bureaucrats in Brussels might ban Zakopane's signature cheese due to its use of unpasteurized milk. Locals feared that their whole way of life would vanish—protests would prepared and politicians badgered. In the end, the humble oscypek received the status of EU Protected Designation of Origin, much like Camembert or Champagne. Providing it comes from the Tatras, and is produced in this way, oscypek is oscypek, Zakopane's favourite salty snack.

The
Savvy Traveler

Before You Go

Government Tourist Offices

In the US & Canada: 5 Marine View Plaza, Apt 208 Hoboken, New Jersey, NJ 07030-5722 (☎ 201/420-9910). **In the UK**: Westgate House, Westgate, London N5 1YY (☎ 08700/675-010).

The Best Times to Go

With a steady influx of low-fare airline passengers, Krakow is Poland's most popular destination, attracting tourists **all year round**. The busiest time is in the **summer**, when the city fills with busloads of tour groups and backpackers. Sudden hot spells can occur but the weather is put to good use with a handful of outdoor cultural events and festivals. **Spring and fall** are more favorable but be prepared for sharp showers. The changing colors of the Planty greenery is a thing to behold in September. **Winters** can be bitterly cold and dark—but the run-up to **Christmas** is wonderfully atmospheric, market stalls and cribs set around the main market square. Poles flood into Krakow for **All Saints' Day**, November 1, and visit the city's cemeteries. Krakow is used as a base to visit the hiking and skiing region of Zakopane—Poles, Slovaks and other foreigners for winter weekends.

Hotel prices drop in the quieter times of year, on weekdays after New Year until March and during November and early December. Prices rise at Easter, for New Year and in the height of summer.

Festivals & Special Events

SPRING. Easter (*Wielkanoc*) is the most important religious festival of the year. Locals enjoy jam doughnuts and sweet pastries before **Lent** and observe a period of fast or lean meals in the run-up to **Good Friday**. On **Palm Sunday**, palm processions take place across the city and churches fill for Mass on **Easter Sunday**. On **Easter Monday** before noon, the men folk splash women with water or cheap perfume, a fertility ritual that may stretch to people chucking buckets of water out of windows.

In **April**, as part of the **Days of Organ Music Festival**, concerts are given in churches across Krakow.

Two public holidays in early May see locals take breaks out of town, **Labor Day** on May 1 and **Constitution Day** on May 3, when a wreath is laid at the Tomb of the Unknown Soldier on plac Matejki. The **Krakow Film Festival** takes place later in the month.

SUMMER. A variety of events and concerts under the umbrella of the **Krakow Festival** is held in squares and public spaces across the city. Locals gather by the riverbank for fireworks on Midsummer's Eve, the **Feast of St John**. From late June until early July, for the **Festival of Jewish Culture** concerts, readings and exhibitions are staged in major venues around Kazimierz. Also in July, the **Krakow Jazz Festival** is held in prominent music bars and cellars in the Old Town.

In August, the main market square accommodates all kinds of performances as part of the **International Carnival of Street Theaters**. Over one weekend, stalls are also set up on adjoining Maly Rynek for food tasting and concerts: the annual **Pierogi Festival**. August 15, the **Feast of the Assumption**, is a national public holiday.

FALL. The biggest event in the local music calendar, **Sacrum Profanum**, calls for performers of major international standing to give shows in industrial and ex-industrial settings across the city. Each year is themed after a certain nation or region—for Germany 2008, Kraftwerk performed at Nowa Huta and music by Karlheinz Stockhausen in the Schindler Factory. Concerts are held over a few days in mid September. For **All Saints' Day**, November 1, a public holiday, cemeteries across the city fill with visitors setting out candles. Ten days later, November 11, Polish **Independence Day** is marked with a Mass at Wawel Cathedral and wreath-laying at the Tomb of the Unknown Soldier.

WINTER. From early December on, nativity cribs and stalls filled with hand-made decorations and local delicacies are set up around the main market square. Masses are held in churches across Krakow on **Christmas Eve**, and on **December 25** and **26**, both public holidays. The market square fills with revellers on **New Year's Eve**—the next day is a national holiday. **Carnival** season also begins from **January 1**, with a series of costumed balls across town, either private parties or organized events in public halls.

The Weather

The local climate is characterized by bitter, long winters, when the temperature can drop to well below freezing, and hot summers, when it can rise to 30 °C and over. Snow is still common in January and February. The air quality is still affected by Krakow's valley location and proximity to the heavy industry in Silesia and nearby Nowa Huta. The smog can be suffocating.

The wettest times of year are spring and fall—be prepared for sharp showers, particularly in September, the wettest month of the year.

Useful Websites

- *www.krakow.pl* The city's official tourism site, with standard information in four languages including English, and a regularly updated list of cultural events.

- *www.visitpoland.org* Useful general site of the UK Polish tourist office.

- *www.polandtour.org* Handy first port of call for North American visitors planning their trip to Poland.

- *www.orbis.pl* Former state-run tourist agency still useful for the practical aspect of traveling and staying around Poland.

- *www.pttk.com.pl* Good for travelers looking to explore the countryside and national parks of Poland.

- *www.judaica.pl; www.jewish.org.pl* These two sites handle all things Jewish in Poland—history, cultural events and attractions.

- *www.cracow-life.com* Local expat site full of tips and information, big on fun and entertainment.

- *www.krakow-info.com* Informative, if somewhat dry, one-stop local database.

- *www.cracowonline.com* Extensive site packed with visitor information. Light on opinion, big on hotel rates and services, tours and festival details.

Cellphones

World phones—or GSM (Global System for Mobiles)—work in Poland (and most of the world). If your phone is on a GSM system, and you have a world-capable multiband phone, you can make and receive calls from Poland. Just call your wireless operator and ask for 'international roaming' to be activated. You can also buy a local SIM card from **Era GSM** (*Ul.Królewska 67*, ☎ *012-623-18-00; www.era.pl*), **Orange** (*Ul.Piłsudskiego 22*, ☎ *012-421-65-76; www.orange.pl*) or **Plus GSM** (*Ul.Królewska 57*, ☎ *012-396-21-50; www.plus.pl*). North Americans can rent a GSM phone before leaving home from **InTouch USA** (☎ *800/872-7626; www.intouchglobal.com*) or **RoadPost** (☎ *888/290-1606 or 905/272-5665; www.roadpost.com*).

Car Rentals

Krakow city centerr is mainly cobbled and pedestrianized—no transport is allowed on the main square. A cheap bus and tram system, and plentiful, inexpensive taxis mean that a car is only necessary if you are going to be making trips in the area—particularly to Ojców and Zakopane. North America's biggest car-rental companies, including Avis and Hertz, have offices in Krakow. The **Avis** office (*Ul.Lubicz 23*, ☎ *0601-20-07-02; www.avis.pl*) office is near the train station. **Hertz** has two offices, one at the Cracovia Hotel (*Al.Focha 1*, ☎ *012-429-62-62; www.hertz.pl*) and one at Balice airport (☎ *012-285-50-84*). Other companies include **EuropCar** (*Ul.Szlak 2*, ☎ *012-633-77-73; www.europcar.pl*), also with a branch at Balice (☎ *012-257-79-00*) and **Joka** (*Ul.Starowiślna 13*, ☎ *0601-54-53-68; www.joka.com.pl*).

Getting **There**

By Plane

From Krakow's **Balice** airport (11km west of the city center) there are three ways to get into town. The easiest is by **train**—a free shuttle bus runs every half-hour from outside Arrivals to the Balice platform. Pay the inspector (6zł) on the train for the 15 min journey to the main train station. The service starts at 4.25am and finishes at 0.10am. The **292 bus** takes a long route to town. A **taxi** costs about 70zł, the fare rising considerably after 10pm.

By Car

Highway **A2** from Germany runs to just north of Łódź, where it links with the **A1** from Gdańsk and the northern coast. This in turn connects with the **A4/8** from Wrocław, which runs east to Katowice and then Krakow. From Warsaw, drive west to pick up the A1 just north of Łódź then continue south.

By Train

Most national (*www.pkp.pl*) and international (*www.db.de*) trains arrive at **Krakow Central** (*Ul.Jana Nowaka Jeziorańskiego 3*, ☎ *012-393-15-80*), the main station just east of the Old Town. Half-a-dozen tram routes stop at Dworzec Główny.

Getting **Around**

By Tram

Trams (*www.mpk.krakow.pl*) circle the Old Town and link it with the suburbs. They are quick, reasonably frequent but often crowded. Ticket machines are placed beside almost every stop. A standard single is 2.50zł, to be stamped on board,

1.25zł for children up to 16. Children under 4 ride free. It costs an extra 0.50zł to buy a ticket on board from the driver. You can also buy tickets valid for one hour (3.10zł/1.55zł) and various passes beginning with 24 hours (10.40zł/5.20zł).

Note that holders of the Krakow Card (50zł for 48 hours, 65zł for 72 hours; www.krakowcard.pl) are entitled to use city transport for the length of its validity.

By Taxi

Most journeys around town should cost under 15zł—the official rate is 5zł plus 2.30zł per kilometer. Taxis should have their number clearly displayed on the sides and the driver must turn on the meter—rip-offs still exist. **Radio Taxi** (9191) and **City Taxi** (9621) are reliable.

By Bus

City buses use the same tickets as trams and mainly serve outlying districts. There are also minibuses, such as the 100 from Salwator to Kościuszko Mound. There is a limited **night-bus** service (5zł) too.

By Car

It is hardly worth bringing a car into the city—although many Poles do. Park at a P sign and buy a ticket from a passing warden. There is a guarded car park at Ul.Westerplatte 18. See p 166 for a list of rental car companies.

On Foot

Strolling in Krakow is an easy pleasure—the city center is compact, grid-patterned and quickly negotiated. Key streets Grodzka, Floriańska and Sławkowska lead to the main market square, Rynek Główny.

Fast **Facts**

APARTMENT RENTALS Scores of companies do long-term rentals in Krakow. You could try: **Krakow City Apartments** (Ul.Szpitalna 34, ☎ 012-431-00-41; www.krakow apartments.info); **AAA Krakow Apartments** (Ul.Cybulskiego 2, ☎ 012-426-51-21; www.krakow apartments.biz) and **Sodispar Service Apartments** (Ul.Józefa 34, ☎ 012-631-26-31; www.sodispar. com).

ATMS/CASHPOINTS Maestro, Cirrus, Visa and Mastercard cards are readily accepted at ATMs all over town—there are half-a-dozen on and off the main square alone. Kantor currency exchange offices are also ubiquitous, with a handful easily found on Floriańska and the main square. Local banks include Bank of Poland, Bank BPH, Bank Ochrony

Środowiska, PKO Bank Polski and Bank Zachodni WBK.

BUSINESS HOURS Krakow keeps the longest hours of any Polish city. While most stick to the regular hours of 10am–6pm weekdays and 10pm–2pm Saturdays, stores stay open much longer at weekends in Krakow, many in the Old Town and main malls keeping weekday hours. Banks, though, open 8am–5pm weekdays and 8am–2pm Saturdays. Many museums close on Mondays. Office hours are generally 9am–5pm weekdays.

CONSULATES & EMBASSIES US Consulate, Ul.Stolarska 9 (☎ 012-429-66-55); **UK Consulate** Ul.Św.Anny 9 (☎ 012-421-70-30).

DOCTORS Dial ☎ 012-422-05-11 to find your nearest doctor.

ELECTRICITY Poland operates on 220 volts AC (50 cycles).

EMERGENCIES For an ambulance or medical emergencies, dial ☎ 999; for fire ☎ 998; for police ☎ 997. The number for all services dialled from a mobile is 112.

GAY & LESBIAN TRAVELERS Homosexuality is legal in Poland but public displays of affection between members of the same sex are not as forthright as they would be over the border in Germany. Krakow now has a couple of gay clubs. The lesbian scene is far more underground. See *www.gay.pl* for more details.

HOLIDAYS National public holidays include: January 1 (New Year's Day); March/April Easter Monday; May 1 (Labor Day); May 3 (Constitution Day); May/June Corpus Christi; August 15 (Feast of the Assumption); November 1 (All Saints' Day); November 11 (Independence Day); December 25, 26 (Christmas).

INSURANCE Check your existing insurance policies before you buy travel insurance to cover trip cancellation, lost luggage, medical expenses, or car rental insurance. For more information, contact one of the following recommended insurers: **Access America** (☎ *866/807-3982; www.accessamerica.com*); **Travel Guard International** (☎ *800/826-4919; www.travelguard.com*); **Travel Insured International** (☎ *800/243-3174; www.travelinsured.com*); and **Travelex Insurance Services** (☎ *888/457-4602; www.travelex-insurance.com*). For travel overseas, most US health plans (including Medicare and Medicaid) do not provide coverage, and the ones that do often require payment for services upfront. If you require additional medical insurance, try **MEDEX Assistance** (☎ *410/453-6300; www.medexassist.com*) or **Travel**

Assistance International (☎ *800/821-2828; www.travelassistance.com*; for general information on services, call the company's Worldwide Assistance Services, Inc., at ☎ *800/777-8710*).

INTERNET Internet access is easily found in cybercafés around the Old Town—most also offer WiFi. A fee of 5zł should guarantee use of a public computer for an hour. Garinet (*Ul.Floriańska 18, ☎ 012-423-22-33; www.garinet.pl*) is central, reliable and stays open until midnight.

LOST PROPERTY If you've left something on a local tram or bus, try the transport office at Ul.Jana Brożka 3, ☎ *012-254-11-50*. Call credit card companies the minute you discover your wallet has been lost or stolen and file a report at the nearest police precinct. Your credit card company or insurer may require a police report number or record. **Visa's** US emergency number is ☎ 800/847-2911—check *www.visa.pl* for Poland. **American Express** cardholders and traveler's check holders should call ☎ 800/221-7282 in the US or check www.americanexpress.com/poland. **MasterCard** holders should call ☎ *800/307-7309* in the US or check *www.mastercard.pl*.

MAIL & POSTAGE The Polish post office (poczta) is reasonably quick and efficient. Post boxes are red. The main office at Ul.Westerplatte 20 (☎ *012-422-39-91; www.pocztapolska.pl*) opens 7.30am–8.30pm Mon–Fri, 8am–2pm Sat.

MONEY The unit of currency is the **złoty**, usually abbreviated to zł. At press time, the złoty was at its strongest in history, approximately 1zł to $0.45.

PASSPORTS No visas are required for US or Canadian visitors to Poland providing your stay does not exceed 90 days. Australian visitors do need a visa. If your passport is lost or stolen, contact your country's embassy or consulate immediately. See "Consulates & Embassies" above. Make a copy of your passport's critical pages and keep it separate from your passport.

PHARMACIES   You should be able to find a standard pharmacy (*apteka*) open during normal business hours around the Old Town, city center, Kazimierz and Podgórze. The details of those on 24-hour duty will be displayed in all their windows. There is also a **24-hour information service** available on ☎ *012-9439* or ☎ *012-422-05-11.*

POLICE   The police (*policja*) emergency number is 997. The number for all services dialled from a mobile is 112.

SAFETY   Violent crime in Krakow is rare, street crime occasional. Ill-lit areas such as the Planty garden ring and around the train station may attract pickpockets after dark but generally the Old Town and Kazimierz are quite safe. Nowa Huta has a bad local reputation but few tourists have any reason to be there at night anyway. There is a 24-hour police station right on the main market square, at number 27.

SMOKING   Walk into a bar and many restaurants in Krakow and the air will be thick with cigarette smoke. Some venues claim to have a non-smoking section but the guidelines are rarely observed or enforced. If you are strongly anti-smoking the only advice would be to come to Krakow in summer, when many venues have terrace seating—or avoid bars altogether.

TAXES   In Poland, most goods carry a VAT tax of 22%. Non-EU residents are entitled to a tax refund on goods bought in Poland and taken permanently out of the EU within three months from the date of purchase. Shops carrying the sticker with the words 'Tax Free Shopping' can help reclaim the VAT levy. The customer must revisit the store in question with the original VAT invoice plus the certificate issued at the border or airport when leaving the EU. Alternatively, agencies such as Global Refund Polska (*www.global refund.com*) do all the paperwork for a certain percentage depending on the purchase amount.

TELEPHONES   For national and international telephone enquiries, dial ☎ *118-912.* For directory enquiries in English, call ☎ *118-811.* To make an international call, dial ☎ 00, wait for the tone, then dial the country code, area code and number. All local calls in Krakow now require the three-digit city code first, **012.** To make a long-distance call within Poland, use the relevant city-code prefix first.

TIPPING   Only the most exclusive restaurants in town add a tip to the bill before it arrives to your table. Otherwise, if you have been satisfied with the service, add the usual 10% or round up to the nearest convenient figure. In cafés and bars, a tip is not expected unless you've been at a place for a long time or the service has been particularly outstanding. For taxi drivers, round up to the nearest convenient figure. A word of warning—if you say 'thank you' as you hand over payment, this can be taken to mean that you are not expecting any change back. If that's not the case, make this clear as you pass the waiter the money.

TOILETS   Public toilets are more in evidence around the city center these days. In places such as the train and bus stations, there may be a nominal fee to pay an attendant. Pictorial signs almost always differentiate the toilets for men and women.

TOURIST INFORMATION **City Tourist Information**, Ul.Szpitalna 25 (☎ *012-432-01-10; www.biurofestiwalowe.pl*) is a little hut in the Planty ring between the Old Town and the train station. It is open in summer 9am–7pm daily, and winter 9am–5pm daily. The regional office, **Małopolska Tourist Information**, is on the main market square at Rynek Główny 1/3 (☎ *012-421-77-06; www.mclt.pl*).

TRAVELERS WITH DISABILITIES
Krakow is quite limited in accommodating visitors with disabilities. Wheelchair access and lifts have been installed at the train station and a handful of attractions—such as the main building of the National Museum—but the cobbled streets of the Old Town are tricky and few restaurants and only a handful of hotels have been converted. You might consider taking an organized tour specifically designed to accommodate such travelers. **Flying Wheels Travel** (☎ *507-451-5005; www.flyingwheelstravel.com*) offers escorted tours to Poland, and **Access-Able Travel Source** (☎ *303-232-2979; www.access-able.com*) has access information for people traveling to Krakow.

TMB (the public transportation system for both bus and Metro) has a help line for disabled travelers (☎ *93-486-07-52*), and ECOM is a federation of private disabled organizations (☎ *93-451-55-50*).

Krakow: **A Brief History**

50,000 BC Evidence of human settlement and activity on Wawel Hill.

1ST C. AD Evidence of trade between Krakow settlers and the Roman empire.

600–1000 Pagan Vistulans occupy Krakow for 400 years.

800 Vistulan power and influence wane; Krakow becomes part of the Great Moravian Empire.

1000 Bishopric of Krakow established.

1038 Kazimierz the Restorer makes Krakow the capital of Poland. Construction begins on first cathedral.

1079 Martyrdom of St Stanysław.

1140S Completion of second cathedral at Wawel. Beginning of first Piast dynasty.

1241 Tartar invasion of Krakow, the first of three. Defensive walls built.

1340S–1360S Kazimierz III the Great rules. Wawel rebuilt in Gothic style. Establishment of the University of Krakow.

1389 Jagellonian dynasty established.

1410 The Battle of Grunwald, or Tannenberg. Polish and Lithuanian armies defeat Teutonic Knights. German expansion prevented.

1470S Veit Stoss works on the altar of St Mary's Basilica. Printing press established.

1491 Nicolaus Copernicus enrols at the University of Krakow.

1504 Rebuilding of Wawel begins. Zygmunt Bell hung. First Renaissance works in Krakow.

1569 Establishment of Polish-Lithuanian commonwealth.

1596 King Zygmunt Vasa moves the royal court from Krakow to Warsaw.

EARLY 1600S Early baroque style established.

1655 First Swedish invasion of Krakow.

EARLY 1700S Later Swedish invasions.

1734 Last coronation at Wawel.

1772–73 First partition of Poland between Austria, Prussia and Russia.

1788 Astronomical observatory established.

1795 Third partition of Poland. Krakow becomes part of Austria.

1800 Wawel becomes an Austrian army barracks.

1809 Krakow part of the semi-autonomous Duchy of Warsaw under Napoleon.

1815 Congress of Vienna. Poland partitioned once more. Krakow independent and neutral.

1846 Krakow Uprising—city back under Austrian rule.

1850 Great Fire of Krakow.

1890S Słowacki Theater opens. Flowering of the arts in Krakow. Modernism and the Młoda Polska movement influential.

1901–05 Palace of Art opens. Stary Theater re-opens in Art Nouveau style. Premiere of 'The Wedding' by Stanisław Wyspiański.

1914 Outbreak of First World War. Polish legions march out of Krakow. Fighting in Galicia.

1918 Austrian Army disarmed in Krakow. Establishment of Polish independence on November 11 after 146 years of foreign rule.

1935 First World War hero Piłsudski given a state funeral in Krakow.

1939 Nazis invasion of Poland, followed quickly by the Soviets. Occupation of Krakow. Professors and intellectuals rounded up and transported to a concentration camp at Sachsenhausen.

1941–42 Establishment of Jewish Ghetto. Development of a death camp at Auschwitz. Oskar Schindler begins employing a significant number of Jews at his factory. Establishment of a work camp at Płaszów.

1943 Liquidation of the Jewish Ghetto.

1945 Soviet troops enter Krakow. After the war, Krakow businesses nationalized, opposition leaders imprisoned.

1949 Construction of Nowa Huta begins.

1979 Karol Wojtyła becomes Pope John Paul II.

1980–81 Solidarity movement established. Protests in Nowa Huta. Martial law declared. Solidarity banned.

1989 Round Table agreements between Communists and Solidarity. Poland leaves Soviet block. Lech Wałęsa elected leader.

1991 Warsaw Pact dissolved.

1999 Poland joins NATO. Papal visit to Krakow.

2004 Poland joins the European Union.

2005 Mass mourning for the passing of Pope John Paul II.

2007 Poland awarded co-hosting of football's Euro 2012 with the Ukraine. Krakow awarded reserve city status.

Krakow's **Architecture**

Romanesque (11th–12th c.)

Original, intact buildings in the Old Town display pristine evidence of this Early Medieval period—most notably **St Adalbert's** church in the main market square and **St Andrew's** church on nearby Grodzka.

Gothic (12th–16th c.)

Gothic emerged in Krakow in the 12th and 13th centuries. The finest example is **St Mary's Basilica** on the main market square, built around the Romanesque original. The **Dominican Church**, begun in 1250, and **St Catherine's** in Kazimierz are further examples. On the northern edge of the Old Town, the **Barbican** and the **Floriańska Gate** show secular use of this architectural style.

Renaissance (early 16th c.)

Italian masters invited to Krakow brought with them the culture of the Renaissance. The most striking example is the arcaded courtyard of the **Royal Castle** at **Wawel. Wawel Cathedral,** originally Gothic, also displays Renaissance touches with the **Zygmunt Chapel,** mausoleum of the Jagellonian dynasty. In the Old Town, the **Sukiennice** in the middle of the main market square shows architectural hallmarks of the Renaissance.

Baroque (17th–18th c.)

Italian masters were also responsible for the prevalence and quality of baroque architecture in Krakow. Completed in 1619, the **Church of Sts Peter & Paul** in Grodzka is early baroque at its best—the High Altar and stucco ceiling above are as magnificent as any baroque creations in Poland. Constructed later that century, **St Anne's** in the University Quarter provides further evidence.

Modernist (early 20th c.)

Work by the key designers and painters of the Młoda Polska movement—**Stanisław Wyspiański** and **Jan Matejko**—can mainly be seen in ecclesistical interiors such as the **Franciscan Church.** The **Hotel Pollera** also contains beautiful Art Nouveau glasswork. The best overall architectural example from this period as a whole is the **Palace of Art** on the edge of the Planty by plac Szczepański.

Socialist & Contemporary (20th c.)

Nowa Huta was laid out according to Socialist planning and retains its features of broad, straight avenues radiating from a central square. Architectural façades borrow from the Renaissance—note the arcaded buildings of Aleja Róż. Also in Nowa Huta, the **Arka Pana** Church shows a bold, contemporary style with its roof in the shape of Noah's Ark.

Useful Phrases & Menu Terms

Useful Words & Phrases

ENGLISH	POLISH	PRONUNCIATION
Good day	Dzień dobry	*djyen' dobri*
How are you?	Jak się Pan/Pani ma?	*yak siye pan/pani ma?*
Very well	Bardzo dobrze	*bardzo dobrzhe*
Thank you	Dziekuję	*djye-kuye*
You're welcome	Proszę	*proshye*
Goodbye	Do widzenia	*do vidjenya*
Please	Proszę	*proshye*
Yes	Tak	*tak*
No	Nie	*nye*
Excuse me	Proszę Pana/Pani	*proshye pana/pani*
Where is . . . ?	Gdzie jest ?	*gdzhye yest?*
To the right	Na prawo	*na pravo*
To the left	Na lewo	*na levo*
I would like . . .	Poproszę	*po-pro-zhye*
I want . . .	Potrzebuję	*po-trje-buye*
Do you have . . . ?	Czy Pan/Pani ma . . . ?	*chi pan/pani ma . . . ?*
How much is it?	Ile kosztuje?	*il-lair kosh-tooye?*
When?	Kiedy?	*ki-yedi?*
What?	Co?	*tso?*
There is (Is there . . . ?)	Czy jest?	*chi yest?*
What is there?	Co jest?	*tso yest?*
Yesterday	Wczoraj	*vchoray*
Today	Dzisiaj	*dji-see-ay*
Tomorrow	Jutro	*yutro*
Good	Dobry	*dobri*
Bad	Niedobry	*nye-dobri*
Better (Best)	Lepiej (Nalepiej)	*lye-pee-yey (na-lye-pee-yey)*
More	Więcej	*vee-yes-sey*
Less	Mniej	*mn-ee-yey*
Do you speak English?	Czy Pan/Pani mówi po angielsku	*chi pan/pani moo-vee po an-geel-skoo?*
I speak a little Polish	Mówię mały Język polski	*moo-vee ma-wee ye-zik pol-ski*
I don't understand	Nie rozumiem	*nye ro-zoo-mee-yem*
What time is it?	Która godzina?	*kt-oora god-zina?*
The check, please	Poproszę o rachunek?	*Po-proshye o ra-hoo-nek?*
The station	Dworzec	*dvor-zets*
a hotel	Hotel	*ho-tehl*
The market	Rynek	*ree-nek*
A restaurant	Restauracja	*rest-ow-rah-see-ya*
The toilet	Toaleta	*toe-a-ley-ta*
A doctor	Doktor	*dok-tor*

ENGLISH	POLISH	PRONUNCIATION
The road to . . .	Droga do . . .	*dro-ga do?*
A room	Pokój	*po-koo-ye*
A book	Książka	*ks-ya-yonzh-ka*
A dictionary	Słownik	*swov-nik*

Numbers

NUMBER	POLISH	PRONUNCIATION
1	jeden	*ye-den*
2	dwa	*dva*
3	trzy	*tzhi*
4	cztery	*chteri*
5	pięc	*pi-yench*
6	sześć	*shesh*
7	siedem	*sye-dem*
8	osiem	*os-yem*
9	dziewięć	*dj-ye-veech*
10	dziesięć	*dj-ye-seech*
11	jedenaście	*ye-den-ash-che*
12	dwanaście	*dva-nash-che*
13	trzynaście	*tzhi-nash-che*
14	czternaście	*chter-nash-che*
15	piętnaście	*pee-yet-nash-che*
16	szesnaście	*shes-nash-che*
17	siedemnaście	*sye-dem-nash-che*
18	osiemnaście	*osyem-nash-che*
19	dziewiętnaście	*dj-ye-nash-che*
20	dwadzieścia	(*dva-djee-sheeya*
30	trzydzieści	*tzhi-djee-shee*
40	czterdzieści	*chter-djee-shee*
50	pięćdziesiąt	*peech-djee-shee-yont*
60	sześćdziesiąt	*shesh-djee-shee-yont*
70	siedemdziesiąt	*sye-dem-djee-shee-yont*
80	osiemdziesiąt	*os-yem-djee-shee-yont*
90	dziewięćdziesiąt	*djee-veech-djee-shee-yont*
100	sto	*sto*

Menu Glossary

Śiadanie	Breakfast
Obiad	Lunch
Kolacja	Dinner
Wegetariański	Vegetarian
jadłopis	Menu
talerz	Plate
Nóż	Knife

widelec	Fork
Łyżka	Spoon
filiżanka	Cup
szklanka	Glass
Gotowany	Boiled
Z rusztu	Grilled
Nadziewany	Stuffed
Pieczeń	Roast meat
Mięso	Meat
Ryby	Fish
Drób	Poultry
Zupa	Soup
Ryzd	Rice
Ziemniaki	Potatoes
Pierogi	Dumplings with various fillings
Chleb	Bread
Warzywa	Vegetables
Surówka	salad
Desery	desserts
Naleśniki	pancakes
Cielęcina	veal
Dzik	boar
Gęś	goose
Golębki	rice and meat in cabbage
Indyk	turkey
Kaczka	duck
Kurczak	chicken
Łosoś	salmon
Pstrąg	trout
Wierprzowe	pork
Wołowe	beef
Ciastko	cake
Lody	ice-cream
Pierniki	soft gingerbread biscuits
Sernik	cheesecake
Cukier	sugar
Herbata	tea
Kawa	coffee
Mleko	milk
Piwo	beer
Sok	juice
Wino	wine
Wino słodkie	sweet wine
Wino wytrawne	dry wine
Woda	water
Woda mineralna	mineral water
Wódka	vodka

Soups & Stews

Barszcz	beetroot soup
Chłodnik	Sour milk, beet and dill soup, cold
Fasólka po Bretońsku	bean soup with bacon
Żur	rye flour soup with sausage and egg
Żurek ż	with potatoes and mushrooms

Dishes of Southern Poland

Kwaśnica	sauerkraut and meat stew
Oscypek	hard, salty local cheese
Strudel jabłkowy	apple strudel
Zalewajka	potato, sausage and mushroom soup

Index

See also Accommodations and Restaurant indexes, below.

Accommodations Index

Restaurant Index

Photo **Credits**

Front Matter Credits: i: © Kevin Foy / Alamy; © Gregory Wrona / PCL; © Donal Mullins / Shutterstock.

All images: © Fumie Suzuki with the following exceptions:

© Crazy Guides: p4 bottom.

Photo **Credits**